The Art of
Kavana

Ignite Your Judaism & Your Life

A handbook for improving kavana and
deveikus Bashem in tefilla
and throughout the day

Rabbi Alexander Seinfeld

DEVORA
PUBLISHING
NEW YORK◆JERUSALEM◆LONDON

The Art of Kavana:
How to Ignite Your Judaism and Your Life
Published by Devora Publishing Company
Copyright © 2009 by Alexander Seinfeld

Please send comments and corrections to seinfeld@jsli.org

COVER DESIGN: Benjie Herskowitz
TYPESETTING & BOOK DESIGN: Koren Publishing Services
EDITORIAL AND PRODUCTION DIRECTOR: Daniella Barak
EDITOR: Dvora Kiel

HARD COVER ISBN: 978-1-934440-27-8
SOFT COVER ISBN: 978-1-936068-00-5

Includes bibliographical references and index
1. Jewish way of life. 2. Meditation – Judaism. 3. Spiritual life – Judaism. 3. Spiritual exercises. 4. Kabbala. I. Title.
BM723.S38   2005   296.7'

Seinfeld, Alexander
The art of *kavana*: how to ignite your Judaism and your life / Alexander Seinfeld

Printed in the United States of America

In memory of

DENNIS GARY SEINFELD

1940–2005

Champion of Justice
Devoted to His Family and to Tikkum Olam

By his loving wife
Karen G. Seinfeld

❦

דוד קאהן

ביהמ״ד גבול יעבץ
ברוקלין, נוא יארק

[Handwritten Hebrew text]

To whom it may concern:

The book of R. Alexander Seinfeld has come to my attention, on topics of *kavana* in *tefila*, to awaken the hearts of Jews to prepare themselves for *tefila* in a way that they should achieve *deveikus Bashem* and they will not act simply out of rote. I have seen in it deep and helpful things and each individual will find in it something relevant to himself.

Signed in honor of those who are *mekaravim Yisroel lAviham Shehb'Shamayim,*

   [HaRav] Dovid Cohen
   2 Kislev, 5769

Shearith Israel Congregation
קייק שארית ישראל
PARK HEIGHTS AND GLEN AVENUES
BALTIMORE, MARYLAND 21215

YAAKOV HOPFER, RABBI
466-3060 Study
358-8281 Residence

יעקב האפפער
באלטימאר, מד.

[Handwritten Hebrew letter]

I have seen your book *The Art of Kavana*, which explains topics of *tefila*, in the context of "things that stand at the height of the world." To speak directly to our Creator and Former as one speaks to a friend, this is "the service of the heart" that the Torah commands us and as our Sages of blessed memory explained to us. How to achieve *deveikus* and how to accomplish speaking to Hashem in a real way is one of the hardest things for us today, and as the Sages expounded in *Talmud Eiruvin* on the verse "drunken but not with wine" (Isaiah 50:1). And it is this problem that our friend Reb Alexander has come to address. I have examined the book and in the places that I looked there were good and helpful words, words that help to internalize the kavana and the feeling of "standing before Hashem"; and "chazaka al chaver sh'ain motzi mitachas yado davar sh'aino m'sukan."

Signed *l'chavod yedidi 'vchavivi* on the 1st day of Hanukkah, 5769, in Baltimore,

[HaRav] Yaakov Hopfer

There is no happiness in this world in material things; there is only happiness in spiritual concerns. The one who enjoys a rich spiritual life is happy. There is no other kind of happiness in existence.

– Rabbi Eliyahu E. Dessler

Contents

Study Schedule. xi
Author's Note xiii
Author's Preface xv

CHAPTER 1   *Getting Started*. 1
CHAPTER 2   *Hashkafa*. 15
CHAPTER 3   *Pleasure*. 33
CHAPTER 4   *Mindfulness* 43
CHAPTER 5   *Appreciation*. 53
CHAPTER 6   *Love and Unity*. 73
CHAPTER 7   *Being Good*. 97
CHAPTER 8   *Creativity* 113
CHAPTER 9   *Virtuosity* 143

ACKNOWLEDGMENTS. 155
ABOUT THE AUTHOR 157

APPENDIX A   *Bibliography* 159
APPENDIX B   *The Exchange* 162
APPENDIX C   *Major Types of Jewish "Meditation"*. 166
APPENDIX D   *Prophecy*. 168
APPENDIX E   *The Seven-Minute Orange* 170
APPENDIX F   *More Berachos* 176

INDEX 178

Study Schedule

This schedule is designed with the assumption that one is doing all of the exercises within each reading segment. This is a fast schedule – one could easily extend each segment to two weeks. Alternatively, it would be possible to condense the schedule into two segments per week, to be completed over approximately eight weeks, for instance from Pesach to just after Shavuos.

Week 1:	Chapter 1
Week 2:	Chapter 2
Week 3:	Chapter 3
Week 4:	Chapter 4 pages 43-48 (until "Developing Constant Kavana")
Week 5:	Chapter 4 pp. 48-51
Week 6:	Chapter 5 pp. 53- 58 (until "Constant Appreciation")
Week 7:	Chapter 5 pp. 58-71
Week 8:	Chapter 6 pp. 73- 78
Week 9:	Chapter 6 pp. 79-89 (until "Level 3")
Week 10:	Chapter 6 pp. 89-96
Week 11:	Chapter 7 pp. 97-106
Week 12:	Chapter 7 pp. 107-111
Week 13:	Chapter 8 pp. 113- 122 (until "Structure of the Amida")
Week 14:	Chapter 8 to 122-138 (until "Ultimate Creativity")
Week 15:	Chapter 8 pp. 138-141
Week 16:	Chapter 9

Author's Note

As an attempt to please everyone, I have followed the Ashkenazic pronunciation in the liturgical references, which most authorities agree is preferable for Jews of European heritage, but use the contemporary Sephardic pronunciation of vowels for the general text. The *ch* is pronounced gutturally: *kh*. Readers who are concerned about the appropriate pronunciation of berachos (blessings) and tefillos (prayers) are encouraged to ask their own mentors.

Author's Preface

Our generation is zocheh (privileged) to witness a spiritual revolution. As in other historical époques, *Klal Yisrael*, the people of Israel, has a central role in this global movement, which is growing slowly but steadily like the dawn. Yet paradoxically, Jewish society appears in some ways headed toward darkness – another tragic downturn in a 3,300-year roller-coaster history.

The apparent problem is rooted in widespread ignorance of Torah. Many factors have contributed to this illiteracy, including an alluring, scientific-materialist culture (in contrast to an unalluring edifice of meager Jewish ritual); a dogmatic popular stereotype of religion (thanks to nearly two millennia of non-Jewish religious fundamentalism); the destruction by the Nazis (*yemachu shemotam* – may their memory be obliterated) of most of the great Jewish learning centers; and the mere effort of survival. These factors have contributed to the disengagement of half or more of the Jewish people from our rich heritage.[1]

What makes this trend especially troublesome from even a

---

1. See Alexander Seinfeld, *The Art of Amazement* (New York: Penguin, 2005), p. 4.

purely sociological perspective is that the typical disenchanted Jew has not found satisfying spiritual alternatives. He has scoured the spiritual marketplace and remained unfulfilled, half-heartedly upholding a few customs at Chanuka and Pesach with some vague sense that he (or his children) may one day discover their deeper meaning.

That day has arrived.

A groundswell of disconnected Jews are now discovering Judaism's best-kept secret: Something is going on in Judaism. It is a reservoir of untapped wisdom. As some have always known, Judaism is a spiritual gold mine waiting to be discovered. The observant reader is challenged to make an even greater effort to make sure that his or her own Jewish practice is neither rote nor routine, but rather transcendental and spiritual.

A new or renewed spiritual journey is difficult to begin and harder to maintain. The present volume creates a structured system to serve as something of a guidebook to the journey. It outlines the ancient Jewish spiritual arts in clear terms for anyone. Each chapter is a stand-alone lesson with step-by-step exercises on how to achieve a particular aspect or level of *kavana*, or spiritual awareness. These levels are progressive, so the ideal approach is to linger at each lesson until completing that set of exercises. Such self-discipline will enable a sincere seeker to use the book as a practical guide to life's subtlest pleasures.

I often describe certain Jewish practices as "meditations," for to live a life of kavana requires a kind of mental discipline and practice that may be called meditative.

Please do not get trapped by any stereotypes you may have regarding meditation, because they are not what this book is about. The book will indeed speak to those seeking meditation but also will appeal to those who seek an enhanced spiritual life without getting into meditation. For if a person makes a *beracha* (blessing), says the *Krias Shema* (a central prayer), or *davens* (prays) with kavana, or performs any *mitzva* (commandment) with kavana, the action becomes *meditative*.

Many individuals have left their indelible marks in this book, either directly or indirectly. First and foremost, Rabbi Noach Weinberg z"tzl, who has created a center in Jerusalem for the promulgation of *Toras Chaim* – practical Jewish wisdom for daily living. Those familiar with Rav Noach's pedagogy will discern his influence on this book.

In addition to Rav Noach z"tzl and the textual sources cited, others who had a significant influence on the development of this book include: Rabbi Yitzchak Berkovitz, Rabbi Dr. Nathan Lopes Cardozo, Rabbi Chaim Uri Freund, Rabbi Moshe Heineman, Rabbi Moshe Shapiro, Rabbi Mordechai Sheinberger, Rabbi Dr. Akiva Tatz, and Rabbi Noson Weisz. Any errors, of course, are my own.

I have constructed the book as a curriculum for both the individual and a class – beginners and the knowledgeable – to begin transforming their lives.[2] To inform this broad audience, the endnotes range from the illustrative to the technical.

Chapter One presents the historical background to this curriculum and to this particular volume. Chapters Two and Three lay the philosophical groundwork necessary to approach kavana arts adroitly – for the mind should understand and then lead the heart and body. Chapters Four through Eight guide the reader progressively through the practices themselves. Chapter Nine unifies the various ideas and practices into a holistic system.

I will consider the book successful to the degree that readers rediscover a Judaism of profound spirituality, a system where familiar rituals and beliefs are gateways to universal *deveikus Bashem*, a concept we will explain later. Even one who already has such a perspective may find this book helpful in deepening the meaning of their practice and sharing it with others.

---

2. The text is intended for an adult reader; for students, it is advised to use with the supervision of mechanchim (educators).

Chapter 1

Getting Started

The Art of What?

- ➤ *Breaking Stereotypes*
- ➤ *What Is Kavana?*
- ➤ *A Brief Historical Background*
- ➤ *Avraham, Spiritual Giant*
- ➤ *Other Key Concepts*
- ➤ *Methodology of This Handbook*

> It's not in Heaven, that you should say, "Who will go up for us to Heaven and get it for us so that we will hear it and do it? Nor is it across the sea, that you should say, "Who will cross the sea for us to get it for us so that we will hear it and do it?" But the word is very near to you, in your mouth and heart to do it.
> – *Devarim* 30:12–14

T ry to remember the most spectacular sunset you ever saw. Picture the setting (likely a beach or a mountaintop); visualize the colors – the oranges and reds, the purples and blues, painted across the sky. How did you feel? Recall the sensation of your mind expanding to the size of the horizon. For at least a moment, perhaps, you felt a tremendous joy, a calmness, and even a flow of energy. Some have felt a sense of timelessness. Others describe a feeling of awe so overwhelming that one gasps – it is literally breathtaking.

Take a few moments to recall such an experience: watching a sunset, downhill skiing, reaching the summit of a mountain, witnessing a birth, or feeling an earthquake. What these moments all have in common is that, however briefly, you really felt alive! You felt a powerful sense of awe or beauty, bigger than yourself; you felt connected, great! You may have even said, "*Wow!*"

Whenever you find yourself saying *Wow!* with your entire being you are experiencing a sort of connectedness that is the aim of this book and the aim of Judaism. Unfortunately, although we all relish such profoundly transcendental moments, they occur spontaneously and infrequently, seldom when and where we choose.

The purpose of this book is to help you identify the source of that amazement, to cultivate it and to experience it daily – even hourly and minute by minute.[1] This practice is the art of kavana, and it is central to all that we do.

● Breaking Stereotypes

In the past century or two, Judaism has been reduced for more and more Jews to a mere assortment of rituals and traditions, like shul and Shabbos, bar mitzvas, Chanuka, Pesach, maybe a dash of ancient history, gefilte fish and Manischewitz wine. The phenomenon of secular Jewish culture is so prevalent that even in the most Orthodox shuls, some one will inevitably ask me, "Are you related to the *other* Seinfeld?" This secularization of Judaism has reached every sacred symbol. The Land of Israel is for most Zionists a secular homeland. Even the Holocaust, once a uniquely Jewish experience, has become for the Shoah Foundation a mere example of the universal problem of genocide.

---

1. Cf. *Shavuos* 39b.

Often those who attempt to make the rituals more meaningful feel stymied by a lack of knowledge and stigmatized because any variation from the group norm is looked on as deviant or radical.

For we have reached such a nadir that "spirituality" for many conjures up non-Jewish images. Thus when Jews do look for spirituality, they often find non-Jewish systems more alluring than what they have seen in Judaism. Don't think that this trend is limited to heterodox Jews. I personally know Orthodox Jews who have incorporated Eastern practices into their daily routine.

One recent example underscores the depth of our ignorance. Despite the fact that the present volume and my previous book are entirely Torah-based, a director of a certain Jewish day school accused me of plagiarizing a Buddhist writer (his letter and my reply are quoted verbatim in Appendix B). What could be worse than a head of a Jewish day school confusing Judaism with Buddhism?

Perhaps equally unfortunate is that masses of people who, genuinely seeking a meaningful spiritual life, are enticed into something called "Kabbala." They take classes and read books about upper spheres and lower spheres and fields of wheat and tulips. They usually feel they are learning something special but don't necessarily feel more spiritually satisfied or make any lasting spiritual change.

This trend has seeped into the observant communities. It used to be sufficient to offer a class on *shalom bayis* (marital tranquility) or perhaps spirituality in marriage. Yet recently I saw a flyer for a class given by a prominent teacher on the "Kabbala of Marriage."

This trend reflects the thirst of all Jews for greater connection. No group, no matter how observant, is exempt. Indeed, sometimes observance poses a hurdle to connection because it can allow a person to compartmentalize his *deveikus* (his connection). In recent years, many *frum Yidden* have made the refreshing discovery that *Yiddishkeit* is meant to be spiritual all of the time, not just in *shul* at *Ne'ila* (the closing Yom Kippur prayers).

3

The art of kavana is practical and accessible to anyone, regardless of his degree of observance or personality. It does not demand a radical lifestyle change. On the contrary, the healthy spiritual path requires very small changes in routine while wrestling with larger shifts in perspective. It consists of many interrelated ideas and practices. One must consider, understand, and try each idea and practice on its own merits. It is not an all-or-nothing system.

The system does require thought. Rather than rely on faith alone, it has a logical framework. Spiritual fulfillment thereby depends in part on one's intellectual grasp of the philosophical model. To this end I have divided the book according to levels of logic, each one building on the last. For this reason it is important to master the first three chapters before tackling the practical tools presented in Chapters Four through Nine. After completing Chapter Three, however, feel free to skip around.

Although this book is primarily addressed to those who are ready to tackle the exercises and grow spiritually, even the casual reader will benefit from processing two important ideas:

- how spirituality and kavana have been integral to Judaism for thousands of years;
- how the art of kavana is arguably Judaism's central purpose.

Some find these two points so compelling that they wonder why they never heard of them before. They wonder how there could be Jewishly active Jews of all stripes who never heard of them. When encountering new and unfamiliar ideas, the reader is encouraged to consult the references in the endnotes and bibliography for enlargement of the discussion.

❧ What Is *Kavana*?

Few people have a good definition for kavana. The word usually conjures up an idea of closing the eyes and concentrating intently.

One definition of kavana is "focused attention." Others define it as a technique for improving one's awareness or attention.[2]

Most of us know someone who has better kavana than we do. We usually associate the image of a *tzaddik* or *tzadeikis* (pious man or woman) the idea of tremendous kavana. What most Jews do not realize, however, is that astounding levels of kavana are available to each and every one of us.

The Torah itself gives us the tools we need to develop our kavana. This development is a discipline. Our success and fulfillment in the discipline depends first and foremost on our grasp of the concepts. The more intellectual clarity we develop, the more we succeed.

One long-term result of improving one's kavana is the development of a mind that is able to focus at will in various settings. This is the most basic mental skill and the secret to success in many human endeavors, such as speed reading, music, athletics, recreational play, and sleep. The benefits to one's spiritual practices are obvious.

❧ A Brief Historical Background

The very idea of Jewish spirituality astonishes many Jews. Even if you are not such a Jew, this section will help you explain the history of Jewish spirituality to others.

Some people are aware of an esoteric Judaism associated with certain mysterious texts such as the *Zohar*. Since most of these were first published in the Middle Ages, there is an erroneous popular belief that Jewish mysticism began then. In reality, meditative disciplines have been part of Judaism since ancient times. Ancient Eretz Yisrael abounded with schools, teachers, and disciples, especially during the First Temple era (ca. 900–500

---

2. David R. Blumenthal, quoted in Seth Kadish, *Kavvana: Directing the Heart in Jewish Prayer*, p. 563.

B.C.E.).[3] These schools were led by spiritual masters known as *nevi'im*, translated as "prophets" but understood more precisely as masters of kavana.[4]

These masters promulgated many techniques, some of which fit our stereotypes and others that do not. Miscellaneous examples include chanting, gazing at a flame, and breathing techniques. One of the advanced methods involves quietly concentrating on certain letters of the Hebrew alphabet. These meditative practices have survived the millennia, passed discreetly from teacher to student (see Appendix C for more examples).

This chain of tradition seems to have originated well before the First Temple period. For instance, the *Chumash* (five books of the Bible) says of Avraham's son Yitzchak:

> *Vayeitzei Yitzhak lasuach basadeh*, "Yitzchak
> went out to 'lasuach' in the field."
> – *Bereishis* 24:63

Commentaries differ widely on the exact meaning of *lasuach*, a word which appears exclusively in this passage. Some say it involves sitting still, others say it means walking, talking or even singing. But nearly all agree that the term is an overt reference to a meditative practice.[5]

The *Midrash* gives a context to Yitzchak's meditation, relating that Avraham, Yitzchak and Yaakov were all steeped in even

---

3. Cf. *Shmuel* 1:19:20–23; there, *Targum Yonasan* interprets *natzav* as *malif* (teaching); see the Radak there. From this passage as well as *Megilla* 14a and Midrashic sources, some infer the widespread, organized study of meditation techniques. See also Aryeh Kaplan, *Meditation and the Bible*, p. 152.

4. Cf. Rashbam on *Bereishis* 20:7. The root *nun-bet-alef* is based on the two-letter root *nun-bet* which denotes hollowness or openness; to receive transcendental wisdom, one must make oneself "open." See also Moshe Chayim Luzzatto, *Daas Tevunos*, p. 331.

5. *Berachos* 26b, *Pesachim* 88a, *Zohar* 39b, *Bereishis Rabba* 60a. Cf. *Torah Temima*.

older wisdom received from Noach's son Sheim. Yaakov Avinu himself spent fourteen years in Sheim's academy.[6] What did they study there for so many years? We're not sure, but various indicators point to astronomy, astrology and some kind of spiritual arts. Regardless of the details, these stories indicate the centrality of the contemplative arts to ancient Judaism.[7]

◆ Avraham, Spiritual Giant

This woven fabric of wisdom and custom sprang from the initiative of one couple, Sarah and Avraham, who died in 1630 and 1592 B.C.E., respectively.[8]

In Jewish spirituality, Avraham was the central stalk from which the flower bloomed. He was a spiritual giant whose greatness can hardly be overstated.[9] He independently discovered the art of kavana and its related spiritual principles. He and Sarah became great spiritual leaders. In their prime, they had thousands of disciples (Avraham taught the men and Sarah taught the women).[10] They were exceedingly wealthy and opened their tent "on all four sides" to welcome every stranger.[11] The Torah gives them a very noble image, like unofficial royalty of the Middle East, "a prince of God in our midst" (*Bereishis* 23:6).

Moreover, Avraham's influence spread to the entire world. He gave his children through Ketura spiritual wisdom, sending them "eastward to the land of the east before he died" (*Bereishis* 25:6). He

---

6. *Megilla* 16b–17a. According to the chronology of *Bereishis* 11, Sheim died when Yaakov was 50; however, Yaakov did not leave home to study in Sheim's academy until age 63, by which time Sheim's grandson Eiver had assumed the leadership.
7. Even those midrashim that are not historically true nonetheless demonstrate that Chazal (our Sages) viewed their own Judaism as deeper than a mere set of rules governing behavior.
8. See Lawrence Keleman, *Permission to Receive*, pp. 90–94.
9. See Ramban on *Bereishis* 40:14.
10. *Bereishis Rabba* 39:14, 84:4, *Sanhedrin* 39b; cf. Rashi on *Bereishis* 12:5.
11. *Bereishis Rabba* 48:9.

became so important for world history that the Torah calls him *av hamon goyim*, "father of the multitude of nations" (*ibid.* 17:5).

This brief background should leave no room for doubt that Judaism has the proper credentials to be our true fountain of spiritual wisdom and any corresponding wisdom in other traditions is exactly that – corresponding wisdom.

✿ Other Key Concepts

SPIRITUAL

The word *spiritual* refers to an experience of the soul as opposed to a material experience of the body. Most of our activities have the potential for both material and spiritual experience. The operative difference lies in our awareness, for the seat of spirituality is the mind. Since most of us interact with the world first and foremost with our bodies, our experiences are always going to have a material, or bodily side. To add the spiritual dimension to an experience, however, requires exercising the mind.

For instance, one can eat ravenously or one can savor food, yet the spiritual act of savoring in no way diminishes bodily fulfillment. Spirituality is very much a state of mind.

Therefore:

- A *spiritual practice* is a regular activity done in order to achieve this state of mind.
- A *spiritual person* is someone whose activities are done with this state of mind.

Consequently both monotheistic prayer and voodoo worship could be spiritual acts. So could creating music, giving *tzedaka* (helping the needy), or teaching a child to read – even eating, shopping, or playing golf. Conversely, all these things, including meditation and prayer, could potentially be devoid of spirituality. Spirituality depends on one's state of mind while performing an action, not on the action itself.

This general definition does not mean that all spiritual practices are equally healthy. Spirituality may be compared to food – some types are conducive to good health and some lead to poor health. Similarly, as with food, we find that the ideally balanced spiritual diet varies from person to person. However, since the soul does not share the body's physical limitations, it is not possible to "overindulge" in healthy spirituality.

MEDITATION

Meditation is a taboo word in the Torah world because it connotes non-Jewish religions, sitting on the floor, eyes closed, perhaps in silence or perhaps chanting. Some equate it with mental stillness. Others associate the word with relaxation. Still others define it as escapism.

In truth, all of the above may be legitimate meditative practices. The common denominator between them is neither the particular form nor the goal, but the action: meditation is a practice that involves *focusing the mind*.[12] Sound familiar?

In other words, doing something meditatively is the same as doing it with kavana. The reason I like the word meditation in a discussion of kavana is because mastery of kavana requires regular practice, like learning music or developing skill in sport. Preferably, one should practice several times a day. The untrained mind constantly adjusts and refocuses. It takes practice to discipline that natural mental function.

This type of mental practice is called meditation. Unlike music or athletics, wherein many of us feel that our physiology prohibits mastery, in meditation the playing field is more level because success has less to do with physiological factors such as the ear- or eye-hand coordination and more to do with willpower.

From a Jewish perspective, it is an interesting fact that the modern Hebrew word for meditation is *meditatzia*, borrowed

---

12. *Encyclopedia Britannica* defines meditation as a "mental exercise conducive to heightened spiritual awareness."

from English. The architects of modern Hebrew used as much of the classical language as possible, and for modern concepts such as airplane or psychology Israelis either invented a new word or borrowed from modern languages, chiefly English. Hence the Hebrew word for airplane is *aviron* from the root *avir* or "air." The Hebrew word for psychology is *psikologiya*, adopted from English. Therefore, since the modern Hebrew word for meditation is *meditatzia*, one might conclude that ancient Israel had no concept of meditation. Why else would modern Hebrew speakers have had to borrow a word?

The contrary is true. Not only did ancient Judaism include a concept of meditation, it was arguably the core concept of Jewish practice. Paradoxically, the lack of a Hebrew word for meditation actually reflects the centrality of meditative practices to Judaism rather than the lack thereof.

This paradox can be explained by a similar phenomenon in arctic cultures. In the Arctic, snow and ice have obvious significance. Consequently, people who live there have developed rich vocabularies for snow and ice. For instance, I found a list of forty-nine words for snow and ice in the West Greenlandic language.[13] If you examine this list, you may notice the paradox: there are no words for "snow" or "ice." Presumably if one were to go to Greenland or Lapland and start speaking about snow in general, one's interlocutor would be puzzled, wondering why you speak so strangely. "What kind of snow do you mean?" he would ask.

We don't find this phenomenon in English because we seem to have words for *everything*. Yet we do have comparable instances in the vernacular. For instance, imagine someone were to say, "Today I'm going to do some movements." We would be puzzled and consider such a statement strange. Then the person might explain, "You know – movements: I'm going to put on special shoes and go outside and move my legs fast." Our response would be, "Oh, you're going to go jogging!" In this example, although we have a

13. Michael Fortescue, *West Greenlandic* (London: Croom Helm, Ltd., 1984).

general word for changing place or position, we nonetheless prefer to speak more specifically.

Jewish "meditation" is comparable to these examples. "Meditation" to early Jews was like "snow" to Eskimos. The lack of a general word does not indicate a lack of the concept. Rather, there are so many kinds of meditative practices that in ancient times a Jew would never talk about them *in toto*. If we were somehow able to ask early Jews about meditation (using a nonexistent catch-all Hebrew word for meditation), they would ask you, "What kind of meditation do you mean?"

Popular meditative arts in classical Judaism run the gamut of forms, including some that resemble our stereotypes of meditation. These include sitting still and focusing on one's breathing, contemplating an object, using a mantra, and so on (see table in the Appendix). The golden age of these disciplines was during the *Bayis Rishon* (First Temple) period (ca. 900 – 450 B.C.E.).

The word kavana is a measure of the meditative quality of what we do. Doing something with "a lot of kavana" or "good kavana" means that the action has great meditative quality. Unfortunately, the same social-political decline that led to the *churban* (utter destruction) of the Commonwealth and the exile of most Jews to Bavel (Babylon) paralleled a spiritual decline. Many were misusing these advanced meditative techniques. They sought spiritual shortcuts, which led them away from the central goals of the Torah and towards *avoda zara* (idol worship).[14]

Even placing aside these hurdles on the spiritual path, fulfillment did not come easy. Advanced techniques require fluency in *lashon hakodesh* (the holy tongue, classical Hebrew) and some actually require one to be physically present in Eretz Yisrael. By the end of *galus Bavel* (Babylonian exile), few Jews spoke He-

---

14. Cf. *Sanhedrin* 64a. The Talmud expounds on *Nechemia* 9:4 as a public acknowledgment that idolatry was the main factor in the destruction [of the Temple]. The Talmud then illustrates the Israelites' former zealous idolatry with several anecdotes.

brew anymore and the Jewish people had been dispersed to many countries.[15]

Consequently, at the close of that historical period the Sanhedrin developed a large set of basic "safe" meditations, such as berachos, by means of which it would be possible for anyone to achieve supreme personal transformation. These basic practices are the foundation of this book. They are easy enough to start using immediately in a meaningful way, yet profound enough for anyone to enjoy years of spiritual growth.

KABBALA

Everyone seems to know what Kabbala is but no one agrees on a definition. Everyone accepts that Kabbala is a body of thought and practice that describes the hidden aspects of reality. The centrality of Kabbala is affirmed in Chumash, when Moshe Rabbeinu is rebuffed in his attempt to encounter the Divine "face to face":

> You cannot see My Face because no one can see Me and live.
> – *Shemos* 33:20

The Torah here is telling us that there is more to reality than meets the eye. Kabbala is a description of the hidden reality and explanation of how the hidden interacts with the observable reality.

This definition will be expanded in Chapter Two.

☙ Methodology of This Handbook

The scope of this book is ancient spiritual practices. Most were transmitted orally for thousands of years before anyone attempted to describe them in writing. Many remain oral to this day.

As mentioned earlier, these practices vary as widely as the arctic snow. From this vast palette, the present volume will cover only the most basic techniques. I have selected those that, through the test of time, have proven to have the widest application. While

---

15. Rambam, *Hilchos Tefilla* 1:1.

stereotypical meditations such as sitting with the eyes closed and focusing on breathing can have an important role, they are not for everyone at every time and place. As I will emphasize in later chapters, ideally, the art of kavana is not confined to isolated moments but nurtured at every instant. Rather than dividing our days into a spiritual part and a material part, we strive to combine the two.

The meditative practices I have chosen to discuss cater to that holistic vision. They provide the reader with a spiritual toolkit that can enable him/her to enhance awareness and deveikus. Although I have designed the program to be user-friendly and self-taught, some guidance or tutoring is preferable. The reader is encouraged to seek the guidance of a master of kavana. Regardless of whether or not one accesses an expert, one can and should seek a chavrusa (learning partner).

> Said Rav Ami: Two scholars who sharpen each other
> in halacha combine [to equal three for a zimun].
> – *Berachos* 47b

If possible, read this book with a chavrusa; at the very least, discuss it with one. You will gain greater levels of insight than you can by learning alone.[16]

This chapter is called "Getting Started" because it outlines the basic vocabulary necessary to proceed. It concludes with three brief exercises to solidify these terms:

---

16. *Berachos* 6a; cf. *Shabbos* 151b.

EXERCISES

1. Define these terms:
    Material... Spiritual... Kavana... Kabbala
2. What is the relationship between meditation and kavana?
3. The following terms have not been defined. What do you think they mean?
    Mysticism... Transcendental

Chapter 2

Hashkafa

Why Are We Here?

- *Bereishis (Creation): Cosmology*
- *Defining Infinite*
- *Purpose of Life*
- *Purpose of Judaism*

The foundation of foundations and the pillar of wisdoms is to know
that there exists a First Existence, causing to exist all that exists.
  – Rambam, *Yesodei HaTorah* 1:1

He also put enigma in [human] hearts, such that no
one can fully grasp the work that God has made.
  – *Koheles* 3:11

Bereishis (Creation): Cosmology

We have always known that the universe had a beginning, because
the Torah begins with this information. However the non-Torah
world was not always certain, and there is an illuminating story
about the scientific discovery of *Bereishis*.

The story begins in 1915 when Albert Einstein circulated a draft of the Theory of General Relativity, also known as the Theory of Gravity. Fatefully, a colleague noticed that these new equations indicated an expanding universe. Einstein found expansion an unacceptable implication of relativity. After all, astronomers at the time overwhelmingly believed what their eyes saw: that we live in a static universe, infinite in time. Consequently, in order to reconcile his new equations with "objective" reality, Einstein adjusted his equations to avoid the implied expansion.

The following decade, American astronomer Edwin Hubble began a revolution in astronomy with his unparalleled 100-inch telescope, seeing farther and more clearly than anyone had ever seen before. Hubble discovered a sort of Doppler-effect phenomenon called "stellar red shift" that proved beyond doubt that the universe is expanding. He published his findings in 1929.

Naturally, Hubble's discovery interested Einstein. In 1930 the great theorist sailed from Germany to California to see the evidence firsthand. On the spot, as a sign of his own greatness, Einstein admitted his error. More telling, he later called his distorted equations "the biggest blunder I ever made in my life." That is a weighty confession. His lapse of rigorous intellectual honesty had led him to miss the historic opportunity in 1915 to reveal through pure thought (mathematics) what astronomy would discover fourteen years later.

It is hard to imagine what could have bothered Einstein so much that he fudged the equations rather than accept the revolutionary idea of an expanding universe. The fact that a scientist "cheated" in order to avoid an uncomfortable conclusion is not particularly remarkable. But when that one scientist is considered one of the great geniuses of the twentieth century, what bothers him becomes very interesting. Some have suggested that the idea of an expanding universe was just too revolutionary for Einstein to believe. Perhaps, however, his Special Theory of Relativity of 1905 ($E=mc^2$) proved that he was not shy of revolutionary or radical ideas.

If the idea itself did not bother Einstein, we are left with only one alternative source for his malaise: the possible implications of the idea. Which implications? We can speculate simply by considering the idea of an expanding universe. If the universe is expanding, then by mentally "rewinding the tape," so to speak, we arrive at the conclusion that the universe as we know it had a beginning.

Today, thanks to Einstein and Hubble, most people accept Bereishis (Creation) as fact. This widespread acceptance is extraordinary in that it completely reverses the scientific view on the nature of nature. Scientists themselves, even more than others, regard Bereishis as a remarkable paradigm shift. Consider the observation of Stephen Hawking, at this writing one of the great living physicists, who called the discovery of an expanding universe a "great intellectual revolution of the twentieth century."

Why does the origin of the universe matter? It may be an interesting theoretical problem, but does it really qualify as a "revolution"? The atomic theory was a great revolution because it teaches that matter – the stuff all around us – is 99.9 percent empty space. This Knowledge paved the way for countless technological innovations. The Special Theory of Relativity led to atomic energy and atomic weapons. Keynesian economics revolutionized the way in which we regulate markets and banks. Psychotherapy has impacted millions of lives. But how has Bereishis affected people personally?

Again, like the expansion, perhaps the most relevant consequence of Bereishis is perhaps what it implies. Maybe the implications are so enormous that even Einstein didn't want to face them. Whether his reaction was conscious or primarily subconscious, we do not know. But we do know that when he altered the equations and delayed the "big bang" theory by a decade, he also delayed humanity's confrontation with all that that theory implied.

❧ Defining Infinite

The biggest implication of Bereishis may indeed have made Einstein uncomfortable, if not as a scientist then as a Jew. For if the universe as we know it indeed had a beginning, any thinking person must ask, *"What came before that?"* It is an unavoidable question. By definition, however, science cannot answer it, for science deals only with what can be observed and/or measured.

While it is beyond the domain of science, this question is at the heart of Judaism. Our Sages, from Avraham until the present, have deeply contemplated the mystery of what came before the universe. They answer that before Bereishis *something* does in fact exist. This something is nearly incomprehensible to us, and the Sages found only one affirmative description for it in our language: unlike existence within the universe, whatever existed prior to *Bereishis* is completely *without boundaries or borders in any dimension.*

Something without limits in any dimension we call "limitless" or "infinite" (or "The Infinite", since there can be only one such entity).

It is important not to confuse this term with mathematical infinity. Mathematical infinity is linear and often defined as a set (e.g., of all numbers). The Jewish concept of "infinite" completely lacks external or internal boundaries.

It is also important not to think of the Infinite Creator as an anthropomorphic being or god. Scrap all concepts of "God" that the Western world has programmed into you. There has been no greater setback for Judaism than Michelangelo's depiction of God as an old man with a long, white beard. Our concept of an Infinite Creator is something beyond the ability of our minds or language to name or define. One of my teachers compared the effort to someone attempting to grasp sounds with his hand. A hand and a sound are in no way compatible.

Even the word *infinite* is a limiting name, because, like all names, it excludes other possibilities. By definition, the Infinite Creator must include all possibilities. But we have no better word than *infinite* to describe that which goes on forever. It seems that, for finite creatures like us, an effort to imagine infinity is no more plausible than my computer appreciating these words as I type them. We're simply not built for that.

Yet we can perhaps get a shadowy glimpse of infinity through analogy. We live on the surface of what seems to be a small planet. Or is it so small?

Imagine that the Earth were the size of a basketball. The biozone, the region that supports all of life on Earth, would be the thickness of a sheet of paper. In other words, from our vantage point the Earth is actually immense! It is so large that the mind has difficulty grasping its size. Our familiarity with globes and maps has tricked us into reducing the Earth in our mind's eye, when in reality it is enormous.

Yet the Earth is minuscule in comparison with the sun – the volume of the sun is 1,000,000 times that of the Earth!

Of course, our sun is a star. Try stargazing on a moonless night. With a clear sky (especially in winter), the whole of our galaxy sprawls brilliantly across the nighttime sky. It is a gorgeous spectacle to behold. Now when gazing at our average-sized galaxy, the Milky Way, remember that our sun is a smaller-than-average star, located near the outer edge of the galaxy. The Milky Way has some 100,000,000,000 stars (10^{11}), most of which are larger than our sun.

But many of what appear to be stars in the sky are actually galaxies themselves, comprising *billions of stars*. How many such galaxies are there? As many as 100,000,000,000 (10^{11}).

When we multiply the number of galaxies by the number of stars in a galaxy, we arrive at the current estimate for the number of stars in the known universe: 10^{22} (in long form that is 10,000,000,000,000,000,000,000). Note that this estimate refers only to the visible universe – who can imagine how far it stretches beyond that?

How do we make sense of a number like 10^{22}? Such a number is, for all practical purposes, absolutely meaningless. Nobody has a grasp of that many stars.

One approach to making sense of it is to compare this number to other large estimates. For instance, estimates for the number of grains of sand on the world's beaches range from 10^{13} to 10^{20}. *This means that there are more stars in the universe than there are grains of sand on all the beaches on earth.*[1] How many more? Not just a few – anywhere from one thousand to a billion times more! That's not just big. That's huge, unimaginably vast – immense. When confronting such a scale, our language falters. And we should not forget that the stars themselves are separated by vast even more expanses of empty space.

Yet we have not even come close to grasping infinity. As unbelievably vast as this universe is, we haven't even begun to scratch the surface of imagining something infinite.

Even more wondrous than that vastness before us is the fact that we are here to contemplate it. Here we are on our lonely little planet, the third stone from a small sun in one corner of one of these billions of galaxies. Of course, our planet is unlike any other stone we know in the cosmos. It is a climate-controlled spaceship, racing through the vacuum of space at thousands of miles per hour. If the Earth were slightly closer or farther from the sun, humans could not live here – we would either freeze or burn. Yet we not only live; in fact, we live well. Consider some of our planet's many extraordinary features:

- perfect chemical elements for life
- abundant natural resources
- a convenient blanket of air to breathe and to keep our temperatures mild
- an ozone layer in the atmosphere to keep out cosmic radiation
- a particular geological history that favored human life
- minimized killer comet and asteroid impacts due to influence of Jupiter

1. The Univ. of Hawaii Department of Mathematics arrived at the figure of 7.5×10^{18}.

- right distance from center of galaxy for heavy elements but minimal cosmic radiation
- perfect orbit to keep water liquid
- large moon at right distance to stabilize tilt.

Could another delicate planet like ours exist in the universe, or are we alone? While the cosmos is unimaginably enormous, there may be no other planet hospitable to complex life anywhere in the universe.[2]

> Almost all environments in the universe are terrible for life. It's only "Garden of Eden" places like Earth where it can exist.
> – Donald C. Brownlee, chief scientist,
> NASA's *Stardust*

From that perspective, stargazing becomes an awesome, speechless experience.

Most people have gone stargazing at one time or another. The stars are clearest and most stunning when viewed far away from city lights. Recall a time when you saw them under such ideal conditions. They were surely very beautiful. And when one stares at them long enough one starts to wonder, *How far does it go?* Well, of course it goes on forever. *But how could it go on forever? There must be an end.* But if there is an end, what's beyond that? *Must be more stars. But how far do they go?* Pretty soon you are either fast asleep or totally confused. But this is a wonderful exercise in trying to grapple with infinity.

> The odds against a universe like ours emerging out of something like the big bang are enormous.... I think clearly there are religious implications whenever you start to discuss the origins

---

2. Peter and Donald Brownlee Ward, *Rare Earth* (Katlenburg: Copernicus Books, 2003).

of the universe. There must be religious overtones. But I think most scientists prefer to shy away from the religious side of it.
– Stephen Hawking, *A Brief History of Time*

Even the greatest imagination falls short because it equates "infinite" with bigness. It is true: by the Jewish definition, the Infinite Creator is infinitely big; or, more accurately, beyond any measure of bigness. But He (She/It?) is also infinitely small – that is, inscrutably precise beyond any measure of smallness. Consider: within a cubic inch of matter there are approximately 10^{22} atoms! Atoms are unimaginably tiny, and we can now measure with precision the size of atoms. *Yet the Infinite – by definition – is immeasurably more precise.*

Too, by definition, the Infinite must also be infinitely beautiful…and frightening…and wise. This Infinite seems infinitely less comprehensible than the linear mathematical definition. How can we understand?

Really, we cannot grasp it. We have to resort to metaphor and our word *infinite* is the best we have. The word *infinite* means "without end." A finite thing has borders, boundaries. Matter is finite. Energy is finite. Time is finite. Our thoughts are finite. Infinity, in contrast, has no ends, borders or boundaries. It goes on forever in every direction in every dimension.

An infinite entity never stops, neither at the planet Earth nor at a human being. By definition, then, this Infinite is everything. It is also everywhere…and all the time (*more accurately, without time*).

Think about what those words imply: *everything, everywhere, all the time.*

The words imply, among other things, that everything we perceive in this world is "part" of the Infinite Creator, even though the Infinite as defined above cannot have parts.[3]

---

3. Rabbi Bachya explains this paradox: "These three attributes are one in meaning and we should see them as one. They do not imply any change

Herein lies a fundamental paradox. How can the universe exist separately from its Infinite Creator? How can the two coexist? For if the Creator is truly infinite, then there should be no finite. Yet we know there is a finite, so how can there be an infinite? How do we conceptualize the relationship between the two?

This fundamental question leads to the second fundamental principle of Jewish philosophy. The first principle is that there is an Infinite that is infinite in every possible way and therefore not bound as we are by space and time.

The second principle can be illustrated with the following metaphor: Imagine yourself at a costume party. Everyone is dressed up: there are clowns, gorillas, one or two Barack Obamas, and so on. Now, imagine one of the gorillas approaches you and says, "Guess who?"

Your response is going to be to look at his height and try to guess: "Dovid!"

"No."

You examine his build more carefully, and guess again: "Chaim!"

---

in God's profound essence, and neither the postulate of randomness nor of plurality of its essence, because what we should understand by them is that the Infinite is neither nonexistent, nor created, nor plural. If we could express the concept of the Infinite with a single word that would in one stroke include these attributes as reason comprehends them, so that these three attributes would come to mind with the use of the one word just as they do when we use the three words, we would employ that word to express the concept. But since we do not find in our spoken languages a word that would indicate the true concept of the Infinite, we express the concept with more than one word" (*Chovos HaLevavos*, vol. 1, 1:10, my translation). Rabbi Bachya also cites Aristotle: "Negatives give a truer conception of the Infinite's attributes than affirmatives" (ibid.). The Alshich HaKadosh seems to learn (*Devarim* 32:9): *Ki chelek Hashem amo* as a reference to the manifestation of an Infinite essence into many finite expressions. (See Alshich on *Shemos* 1:1; available in English: Rabbi Moshe Alshich, *Midrash of Rabbi Moshe Alshich on the Torah*, trans. Eliyahu Munk (New York: Lamda, 2000), p. 339).

"Nope."

You analyze his voice and guess again: "Sender!"

"You got it!"

Now, what is Sender going to do after you guess correctly? Of course, he will take off the mask.

Our rabbis explain that this universe is Hashem's *mask*, a finite facade masking its true infinite nature. For those who pursue Jewish spiritual practices long enough to recognize the reality behind the mask, the mask is removed.[4]

EXERCISES

1. Meditative posture and contemplating eternity (this exercise works best if you have someone read the following paragraphs aloud while you follow the instructions):

   To prepare for meditation, sit in a comfortable chair (or on the floor, if more comfortable), with the back straight and shoulders relaxed. Close your eyes and let your breathing become steady. Lift your right foot and rotate it three times. Repeat with your left foot. Lift your right hand and make a fist for three seconds. Repeat with your left hand. Rotate your right shoulder three times, then your left. Finally, stretch your head to each side for three seconds, then downward. Keeping your eyes closed, you are now in a basic meditative state.

---

4. Rabbi E.E. Dessler, *Strive For Truth,* Trans. from the Hebrew; *Michtav MiEliyahu* by Rabbi Aryeh Carmell (Jerusalem: Feldheim, 1978), vol. II, pp. 236–251; Tatz, *World Mask* (Jerusalem: Targum, 1995), ch. 2–3. Compare this traditional teaching with modern cosmology: "The physical world can be for all measurable intents and purposes infinite, but this infinity is hidden from us as thoroughly as though it were stuffed inside a black hole" (Dr. Sten Odenwald, *Ask the Astronomer*).

To contemplate eternity: while keeping the eyes closed, try the following visualization technique taught by Rabbi Dessler:

> Imagine the ocean…and the beach…and on the beach there is an enormous pile of sand…the highest in the world. It comes to a perfect point at the top. There is no wind, no noise. Suddenly, from over the ocean, a great bird arrives, flies up to the top of this enormous pile of sand, picks up one grain of sand in its beak, and flies back over the ocean. Then a thousand years pass, when nothing happens; no wind, no rain, the pile of sand remains as it is. Then, after a thousand years, another enormous bird arrives from over the ocean, flies to the top of this enormous pile of sand, removes one grain, and returns whence it came. Another thousand years pass during which nothing happens to the pile of sand. Then, after a thousand more years, another bird arrives from over the ocean, flies up, removes a single grain of sand, and flies back over the ocean. How many thousands of years will pass before there will be a noticeable dent in the pile of sand? And how many eons upon eons will pass before the pile of sand is reduced to nothing? When you begin to imagine this vast, vast expanse of time, you haven't even begun to scratch the surface of eternity.[22]

2. Contemplate the infinite-finite relationship. Metaphorically, the Infinite Creator may be compared to light. When passed through a prism, white light separates into seven colors. These distinct colors represent the physical, finite universe. However, there is only one source of light and only one essential light. What we perceive is the result of a filtering process.

    Picture the prism in your mind's eye. Contemplate the symbolism for the natural and the Infinite Light.

Why was the universe created? Due to the insurmountable barrier between our finite minds and God, we cannot know if there might be what we would call a motive for the creation of the universe, and if there was, we have no basis for understanding what that motive might have been. Our concept of motive implies something needed, hence lacking; yet by our current definition, something infinite does not lack.[5] Rather, instead of discussing motive, Jewish philosophy addresses this question in terms of the universe's function.

First, our definition of *Infinite* needs fine-tuning. It is not precise to say that God lacks nothing. In fact, there is one thing that, by definition, the Infinite Creator does lack: *finiteness*. In other words, by saying that God has no lack – we acknowledge that He lacks "lack"!

But how can something simultaneously lack and not lack?

Consider the same concept via a different description: According to Judaism, the Infinite Creator, being infinite, includes in His essence every possible nuance of what we call goodness. One such attribute is the quality of giving. But, by definition, giving requires both a giver and a receiver. How can Hashem express or actualize the quality of giving? Who or what is there to give to, when Hashem by definition is everything, everywhere, all the time?

The only possibility of infinite giving is for Hashem to create a receiver "within" His infiniteness, as it were. In order to do so, He "contracts" some of His infiniteness to make "room" for the finite universe. Kabbala calls this phenomenon *tzimtzum*, which some interpret as "covering" His infinite essence, since by definition He cannot become any less infinite.[6] Since we are finite we

---

5. *American Heritage Dictionary* defines motive as "an emotion, desire, physiological need, or similar impulse acting as an incitement to action."
6. See Rabbi Shneur Zalman Liadi, *Likutei Amarim Tanya*, "Shaar HaYichud" ch. 5–7. His discussion is based largely on the Arizal's (Rabbi Yitzchak Luria, *Kisvei Ari*) interpretation of the first chapter of *Zohar*.

cannot fully grasp this process and any description of it is going to fall short. But that essential infinite quality of *giving* is, according to Judaism, the purpose of Bereishis and of our existence on this planet. Bereishis is (or "was", from our time-bound perspective) the ultimate expression of "giving." This world is Hashem's gift to Himself (so to speak) – He created a lack in order to fill the lack![7]

This model resolves the paradox – not how, but why something would simultaneously lack and not lack. The answer is: in order to give. Infinite altruism. Contrast this description with a human altruist: People who give do so because in that particular situation it feels better to give than not to give. In contrast, the Infinite Altruist gives with absolutely no possibility of receiving anything in return.

Incidentally, we have received from *Chazal* a detailed description and explanation of how an Infinite Creator and a finite creation coexist and interact. This tradition, mentioned briefly above, is called "Kabbala," the chief work of which is the *Zohar*. For the average person to open the *Zohar* and start reading would be analogous to a person who doesn't know arithmetic to read a treatise on quantum mechanics. The wisdom is potentially available to all, but there are prerequisite steps to take. To master the art of kavana is to learn the arithmetic of Kabbala.

➥ Purpose of Life

It should now be clear that every particle in the universe, including we who comprise the most complex arrangements of particles in the universe, has a definite purpose. Our purpose, quite simply, is to receive – to receive goodness or happiness; to receive pleasure.[8]

7. This is a basic understanding of "He created the world only for His glory" (*Avos* 6:11).
8. Luzzatto, *Daas Tevunos/The Knowing Heart: The Philosophy of God's Oneness*, p. 17; *Mesillas Yesharim/Path of the Just*, p. 17.

Herein lies Avraham's great, historic insight. The *Midrash* tells us that as a child, Avraham looked around and saw a magnificent, intricate world. *Where did it come from?* he wondered. Nothing comes from nothing, and surely nothing so beautiful and complex, he reasoned. He considered the dominant belief in Mesopotamian society that the heavenly bodies are the source of existence. But, he objected, if the world came from something finite, where did the heavenly bodies come from? Somewhere back in the chain of cause and effect there must have been something infinite that started it all!

The idea of an unmoved mover that caused the universe was not itself an original thought. Others had the same knowledge. The Torah itself mentions several such people, like Noach, who predated Avraham. Avraham, however, arrived at this conclusion independently within a polytheistic society. Moreover, he carried the logic a step further: "If the Creator is indeed infinite, then by definition 'It' must not lack anything. *Infinite*, after all, means that it has no limits, no lack. But if it has no lack, it could not have created this universe for itself. Therefore, he concluded, it must have created this universe for us! For our benefit, for our pleasure!"

Hence, with a profound grasp of human purpose, Avraham resolved to seek all of life's pleasures, both the material and the spiritual. He recognized that there is actually a hierarchy of pleasures and that the higher pleasures can offset the lower ones. He and Sarah developed wisdom on how to attain the highest pleasures, including deveikus. They transmitted this wisdom to their children and grandchildren; it was taught to Moshe Rabbeinu, and it survives until today in the various texts we call Torah.

❧ Purpose of Judaism

Avraham's goal – the pursuit of pleasure or happiness – remains the essence of Judaism. This idea comes as a surprise to many people and is easily misunderstood. Most of us have two common misconceptions: that spirituality is concerned only with higher-order experiences of the intellect and emotions; and that pleasure means hedonism. Rather, this philosophy does include physical pleasures, that is, any experience that a person enjoys with one of the five senses: smell, touch, taste, sight or hearing. Judaism views physical pleasure as central to living a good life. Hashem made a physical world not to frustrate us but for us to enjoy.

In fact, the tradition considers it a moral obligation to enjoy life's physical pleasures. We learn this from the very first mitzva of the Torah. What is the Torah's first mitzva? It is not "Be fruitful and multiply." Nor is it "Do not eat from the Tree of Knowledge." On close reading, the text plainly states that the very first mitzva is "From every tree of the garden you must eat."[9]

Judaism is first and foremost a system of enjoyment – qualified and disciplined perhaps, but real enjoyment nonetheless. Therefore Judaism considers it a mistake, for example, to refuse an opportunity to taste a new kind of fruit.[10] The concept may be compared to being served dinner at home: When your parent, spouse or roommate prepares a new, exotic food, you may very well wish to pass, but your refusing at least to try it will surely tarnish the relationship.

9. *Bereishis* 2:16. This interpretation is a departure from Rashi but is supported on several counts: the doubled verb "eating you shall eat," which indicates an intensity often translated as "surely"; the position of the verb "commanded" before the positive, and the negative command's position in the subsequent verse, as well as the sources cited in footnote 8. See the Gr"a (Vilna Gaon) in *Ederes Eliyahu*; Rabbeinu Bachya; Rabbi Nasan Tzvi Finkel, *Ohr HaTzafon* 1:2; and *Meshech Chochma*.
10. *Yerushalmi Kiddushin* 4:12, at the end. Cf. *Mishna Berura* 225:19. Compare the *Mishna* in *Sanhedrin* 37a: *kol echad ve'echad chayav lomar, bishvili nivra ha'olam*, "Each and every person must say, 'The world was created for me'" (see also the famous statement of Rabbi Eliezer Hakapar in *Nazir* 19a, and elsewhere).

EXERCISE

3. Are you a total connoisseur of aesthetic pleasure? Use your senses: notice colors, smells and shapes. Appreciate the details of the world around you. Start a journal of your senses and keep a record of what new things you notice. Note five new points of awareness every day for one week.

Yet, one should avoid equating pleasure with hedonism. Pleasure refers to all kinds of pleasures (detailed in the next chapter). We have the ability to derive pleasure from everything we experience in this life: every pencil, every penny, every gum wrapper, every computer, every flower, every person, every moral dilemma, and every project.

Take the time to review these ideas until they are clear. The major part of this book deals with the practical application of this hashkafic (philosophical) foundation. Therefore, because it is important to have a solid theoretical foundation, it may be beneficial – perhaps even necessary – to return occasionally to this chapter for review.

In the words of Dr. Gerald Schroeder, an observant Jew who happens to be a nuclear physicist, once we grasp the concept of a transcendent Infinite Creator and Sustainer of this mask we call the universe, we can take the next step:

> [We can then] investigate how we might capture the all-too-rare rush of joy sensed when we chance upon the transcendent. Instead of waiting passively for it to happen, imagine being able to have that joy a permanent partner in life. That would be called getting the most out of life.[11]

11. Gerald Schroeder, *The Science of God*, (New York: Simon & Schuster, 2000) p. 89.

To take this next step, to begin to grapple with the Infinite Creator, is the historical essence of being a Jew, or more precisely, a *Yisrael*. *Yisrael* can mean "one who grapples with the Infinite." The first appearance of this name in the Torah is at the conclusion of Yaakov Avinu's all-night wrestling match with an angel. The match is a draw[12] and before the angel leaves, he says, "Your name is now Yisrael, because you've wrestled with God...and you've done well."[13]

The metaphor is clear: *Bnei Yisrael* – the Children of Israel – are the heirs to Yaakov Avinu's struggle. We do not relate to the struggle as a literal wrestling contest but rather as a mental and emotional search for the ultimate wisdom and experience.[14]

EXERCISES

4. Based on this chapter, what is Judaism? (Fill in)

   _____

   _____

   _____

5. Reread this chapter as many times as you need to until you fully grasp the concepts. It is tempting to proceed before struggling to achieve total clarity, but understanding subsequent chapters depends largely on absorbing this one.

> Make your ears attentive to wisdom, incline your heart to understanding; only if you call to understanding and give your voice to discernment...if you seek it like silver, and like treasure search it out, then you will understand awe of Hashem, and knowledge of His manifestation you'll find.
> – *Mishlei* 2:2–5

12. *Hizkuni.*
13. *Bereishis* 32:29. See p. 82 note 10 for detailed discussion.
14. See *Onkelos* to *Bereishis* 32:29.

Chapter 3

Pleasure

The Art of Kavana

- ✦ *Body, Soul and Kavana*
- ✦ *The Pleasure Wave*
- ✦ *Mind Control and Meditation*
- ✦ *Prophecy: Ultimate Kavana*

> The real wonder is that God grants us an accumulation
> of memories and prior consequences, as though there
> were any continuity with yesterday's existence. In reality,
> though, such a continuation does not exist: each moment
> is a new existence, literally a creation ex nihilo.
> – Rabbi Yaakov Weinberg, zt"l

Chapter Two defined life's purpose as enabling God to give goodness and pleasure, and Judaism as a system for receiving that gift.
Some find this perspective astonishing and they react in one of
two ways. Some are highly receptive – "It sounds too good to be
true, but if that's what life is for, who am I to argue?" Others are

skeptical – "If it is true, why is there suffering in the world? And why is Judaism so difficult?"

These two reactions are examples of the cliché about a glass being half empty or half full. One can choose to see life as essentially painful (with some pleasure mixed in) or essentially pleasurable (with some pain mixed in). Both the optimist and the pessimist have the ability to receive and to cultivate the pleasures offered us. The only prerequisite is the wisdom to discern real pleasure and to cultivate it.

Unfortunately, our schools do not teach this wisdom. We can spend years learning to create wealth but rarely study how to enjoy it. We can pour enormous resources into a wedding yet never investigate how to give and receive love. Every year Young people spend millions on looking good but little on learning how to be good. After a lifetime of "productive" labor we often leave the world worse than we found it.

In short, we find ourselves living in a world where materialism and ego dominate rather than spiritualism and altruism. This dominant cultural trait runs counter to the Jewish ideal of pleasure. But if Judaism advocates pleasure, what is wrong with materialism? Isn't materialism a legitimate form of pleasure?

We answer these questions by differentiating between material and physical. *Physical* refers to aesthetics: the pleasures of the senses. Aesthetic pleasure is an important part of life, along with *emotional*, *moral* and *creative* pleasures. Judaism not only advocates the pursuit of these four areas of pleasure, but also considers it an error to deny one or more of them, as they are part of our life's purpose.

We experience each of these four areas as either a material pleasure or a spiritual one. A material pleasure is the enjoyment experienced by the body. A spiritual pleasure is the enjoyment experienced by the soul.

❧ Body, Soul and Kavana

This confusion between physical and material results from different theories of the nature of self. Modern culture defines the self in material terms. If my being is essentially material, then my values will be materialistic. Conversely, if my being is essentially spiritual, then my values will be spiritual ones.

Judaism claims that a person is essentially a soul temporarily fused to a body. The soul is a "spark" of the Infinite Source. Just as the Infinite Source is the quintessence of reality, the human soul is permanent and real. In contrast, the body, a product of the finite material world, is ultimately unreal.

Therefore, the extent to which an experience gives pleasure to the soul is the extent to which it is a "real" pleasure; the extent to which it gives pleasure to the body is the extent to which it is unreal.

Every type of real pleasure has an unreal counterpleasure. For instance, one of the most basic pleasures we know is the enjoyment of good food. A gourmet is a person who has cultivated the aesthetic appreciation for food. This is a spiritual pleasure, for although the body is involved, the actual location of enjoyment is not identifiable within the body. Who knows why many people prefer a fine wine with their meal to a glass of water? We might be able to reduce the wine to its elements, see how the molecules affect the palate, yet we would be no closer to understanding why we enjoy drinking it – a sure sign of a spiritual pleasure. Even one day when phrenologists can identify the exact electrical-chemical activity in the brain that occurs when a person enjoys good food, we still will not understand *why* we enjoy the food.

The antithesis of a gourmet is the person the French call a "*gourmand*" – one who eats gluttonously, for bodily satisfaction. There is a constant, unrelenting tension between the two. At any moment, one could choose to unleash the body and devour a chocolate cake. That we have all been there so many times fathered the expression "the cookies were calling me." There *was* a voice calling you to eat the cookies – the voice of your body.

The secret to gourmet eating is to use the body's appetite to energize the eating experience under the control of a disciplined mind. Like a horse and rider, the ideal relationship is that in which the rider is in control. The horse (the body) provides all the power (in this case, appetite) and the rider (soul) all the direction. The mind makes choices at nearly every waking moment of every day to fulfill the desires of either the body or the soul. Ideally, one would strive to discipline the mind to make soul-choices rather than body-choices, to be a gourmet rather than a gourmand.

A useful litmus test to know whether a particular choice is being guided by the soul or by the body is to ask, "Is this pleasure that I'm seeking a short-term gratification (e.g., I'm hungry, I want food now) or longer term (I'm going to take an hour to prepare a gourmet meal in order to savor complex aromas and flavors)?" In fact, it is possible to satisfy both body and soul at the same time. But to do so requires that the mind mediate between the two to prevent the body from running out of control. Unfortunately, exercising the brain comes second only to physical exercise on the list of most detested things to do. This aversion is perhaps why great creativity is so rarely found.

> When Rabbi Yehoshua died, *eitza* (counsel)
> and *machshava* (thinking) ceased.
> > – *Sotah* 49b

> People will go to any amount of effort to
> avoid the labor of thinking.
> > – Thomas Jefferson

> Most people would rather die than think – and most do.
> > – Bertrand Russell

Food and its physical consumption is not the only stage of the soul-body dichotomy; it applies to all kinds of pleasures:

- aesthetics v. gluttony
- love and caring v. lust and infatuation

- ethics v. public image
- creativity v. power.

The words on the left are the spiritual soul-pleasures and the words on the right are the material body-pleasures. Every human experience falls into one of the above four dichotomies. We must constantly negotiate between the material (body) and the spiritual (soul) impulses. The following table illustrates these impulses with messages that typify the competitive pulls of body and soul:

CONFLICTING MESSAGES FROM BODY AND SOUL		
Drive	*Material/ body message*	*Spiritual/ soul message*
Aesthetic	"Let's eat!"	"Make a gourmet meal!"
Love (relationship)	"Touch!"	"Cultivate the relationship!"
Ethical	"Save face/ look good!"	"Do the right thing!"
Creative	"Be successful!"	"Change the world!"

The most important thing to remember is that these messages are constant, like a flowing stream. The body *always* wants material gratification and the soul *always* wants spiritual gratification. Just to be mindful of the dichotomy can have lasting spiritual benefits.

Now, as good as it can be, spiritual gratification is not necessarily *transcendental*. One may experience the most sublime aesthetic, loving, ethical and creative pleasures and never transcend the finite realm. Although they are soul-pleasures, the soul itself remains, after all, attached to the body in this world. Because of the soul's infinite root, however, it has the potential to transcend the boundaries set by the finite world. It can do so within the scope of any of the various pleasures. One can, in other words, infuse one's life with transcendental awareness. Such awareness is a unique pleasure in that by definition it transcends all else. This experience is the experience of deveikus. Striving toward it is the art of kavana.

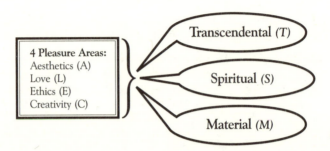

Each item in the box is a realm of pleasure. Kavana is the vehicle for transforming any and every pleasure from a materialistic experience to a spiritual one and even a transcendental one.

Notice how the contents of the physical world (including the body) are necessary agents of spiritual and transcendental experiences. Without the physical, we would be unable to experience transcending it. For example, consider the enjoyment of a sunset. The aesthetic pleasure experienced by my soul cannot happen without eyes to see and a sun to be seen. Because my soul is fused to such a body in such a material world, it is able to experience the aesthetic and transcendental pleasures.

This transcendental access is available via all four areas of pleasure. Any of these four areas affords the possibility of all three dimensions of pleasure: Material, Spiritual, Transcendent.

Subsequent chapters will cover each of the four pleasure areas to show how this process works. The reading should be accompanied by doing the practical exercises. Reading this book without doing the exercises would be akin to reading about Beethoven's Ninth Symphony without ever hearing the music – fascinating, but not transforming.

❧ The Pleasure Wave

The wave model illustrates the above principles with the added element of hierarchy. For, even in the realm of true spiritual pleasure, some pleasures are greater than others.

First, consider aesthetic (sensory) pleasure (A): the diagram represents the fact that one can experience a real (meaning *spiritual*) aesthetic pleasure for itself but can also use that experience to achieve transcendental pleasure. So it is too with the pleasures of love (L), ethics (E). and creativity (C).

The diagram further represents the fact that the soul's experiences of sensory (aesthetic), emotional, ethical and creative pleasure are increasingly more expansive: they attain increasingly "higher" or "greater" levels of pleasure.

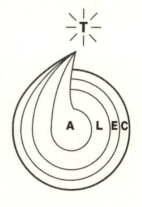

I would like to preempt one point of doubt that often arises. A person who has been raised in the modern world may object to the relatively low status of love on this chart. "But I thought love was the ultimate!" you may object. Sit tight: this challenging point will be demonstrated in subsequent chapters. The chart does not show the *process*, that of the metaphorical rider taming the horse. Without a rider, the horse (body) runs rampant. Under control, it can take the soul on an awesome journey. The mind must continually choose between following the body's inclinations to wander into the pastures of materialism or to stay on the path the soul illuminates.

☙ Mind Control and Meditation

Based on this framework, the pursuit of pleasure depends on the simple mental process of distinguishing between material and spiritual impulses (M and S) and on the conscious choice as to which impulse to heed.

The remaining chapters will each focus on one pleasure area (A, L, E, and C): how to distinguish between the M and S of that area and the tools that Judaism gives us to stay on the spiritual path by consistently choosing S over M – which is the art of kavana. For, as we will see, it is this very tension between spiritual and material impulses that makes the deepest kavana possible.

In order to navigate among the competing messages of body and soul (material [M] and spiritual [S]), we make conscious mental choices. Therefore the foundation of pleasure and the basis of Jewish spirituality is the discipline of mental control, of focusing the mind at will (kavana). To develop kavana requires a systematic development of mental focus, also known as meditation.

> When a person meditates on these things and recognizes all the creations – from forces, to constellations, to people like oneself – he will be in awe of the wisdom of the Hidden Source in all of His handiworks and all His creations. Pleasurable identification with God will increase, and one's soul will expand and one's body will strive to love Hashem, the Source.
> – Rambam, *Yesodei HaTorah* 84:12

Jews of antiquity understood this role of meditation in spiritual growth with such clarity that meditation became as integral to early Israelite culture as television has become to ours. Jews learned meditative practices in schools all over ancient Israel.[1] As these practices developed over the millennia, the ultimate goal has remained the same – to lift one's consciousness beyond the

---

1.   See Chapter 1, footnote 4.

mundane, finite here-and-now and rise toward the Infinite Source of the mundane.

The ancient meditation schools used a curriculum that was specifically tailored toward the achievement of a clear and direct line of communication with God. Such a level of communication is the ultimate state of transcendental awareness and is called *nevius*, or prophecy.

❧ Prophecy: Ultimate Kavana

Prophecy is generally misunderstood. It does not mean simply telling the future. Telling the future *per se* is generally considered an "un-Jewish" practice.[2] Since the greatest Jews in our history were prophets, they must have been doing something other than (or in addition to) predicting the future. Part of the misunderstanding comes from the fact that *Tanach* (Jewish Bible)[3] records the prophecies of only forty-eight post-Mosaic prophets, many of whom bring tidings of doom and destruction. No wonder the word *prophet* has become associated with prescience.

Prophecy is defined rather by an experience than by a specific type of pronouncement.[4] We actually know very little about the prophetic experience because full prophecy has been absent from the world since the fourth century B.C.E. Yet the scattered evidence, including descriptive sources, indicates an experience of channeling energy (see the Appendix for some of these sources).

The average (non-prophetic) person receives indirect but potentially clear communications from Hashem cloaked in the form of the events that occur to us every day. There are some, particularly certain insane people, who can apparently receive direct but unclear communications.[5] In contrast, the prophetic experience

2.   *Vayikra* 19:26, 31; *Devarim* 18:10–11.
3.   *Tanach* is an acronym: Torah (*Chumash*), *Nevi'im* (Prophets), and *Ketuvim* (Writings).
4.   See Lawrence Keleman, *Permission to Receive*, pp. 90–94.
5.   *Baba Basra* 12b.

41

is described as a communication that is both clear and direct. To reach the prophetic state of consciousness required a long period of study, meditation and inner purification. Success required required both tremendous self-discipline and professional guidance. Modern authorities such as Rabbi Joseph Soloveitchik affirm that prophecy is the "ultimate peak" of human creative achievement.[6]

The nationwide system of kavana schools produced, over a period of 500–800 years, over one million prophets – 1,200 or more "graduating" every year.[7] This continual influx created a cadre of prophets who acquired an important social role. Imagine, for example, that you had lost your keys. You would have been able to go to the neighborhood prophet for help. He or she might tell you, "Your keys are in your coat pocket. By the way, you've been careless lately – perhaps you should think about why you lost them in the first place?"[8] In other words, a person who reached the kavana state called prophecy took on a special responsibility to help others grow too.

Each of us has the potential to achieve prophecy.[9] This handbook alone will not get you there, but the basic skills taught in these lessons are the prerequisite for the journey. The first step is to develop the kavana powers of the mind.

6. *Halachic Man* (Jewish Publication Society, 1991), p. 130.
7. This figure is my own estimate based on the Talmudic estimate of the total number of prophets in history (*Megilla* 14a; see p. 6 FN 3). If there were 1,000,000 prophets from Moshe Rabbeinu to the destruction of the First Temple (a period of about 800 years), then there should be roughly 1,250 new prophets every year, on average.
8. Thanks to Rabbi Shmuel Silinsky for this analogy.
9. *Avodah Zara* 20b. See Bamidbar 11:29; cf. Luzzatto, *Mesillas Yesharim (Path of the Just)*, p. 13.

Chapter 4

Mindfulness

Hisbonenus and Deveikus

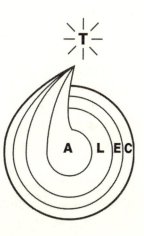

- *Prepare the Body to Prepare the Mind*
- *Focusing the Mind – Contemplation*
- *Developing Constant Kavana*
- *Deveikus*

What is the way to fulfill the mitzva of loving God? When a person meditates (*hisbonenus*) on His deeds and His amazing creations and he realizes His priceless and endless wisdom, he will immediately love and praise and exclaim and desire a great desire to know the great Name.

— Rambam, *Yesodei HaTorah* 2:2

☙ Prepare the Body to Prepare the Mind

The first practice of meditative discipline is, surprisingly, physical: washing the hands. The idea is to clean the hands both physically and ritually. Physical cleanliness requires, of course, soap and water. Ritual washing comes after physical cleaning. The hands should be free of dirt and other things that inhibit the water from contact with the skin.

What is the meaning of this ritual?

The hands are the main link between our bodies and the world around us.[1] They are, according to anthropologists, one of the primary physical characteristics that distinguish us as humans. We use our hands for most physical activities. As our primary physical tool, we relate to our hands in a very physical way. In this context they represent the opposite of spiritual growth. Moreover, because of their constant use they frequently become soiled. Therefore, ritual hand-washing is an act that declares, "I'm stepping into a spiritual realm now; I'm going to elevate my physical body and actions to a higher plane of consciousness." The custom is to wash at key moments of transition between physical and transcendental, such as upon waking, before eating a meal and before certain kinds of meditation and prayer.[2]

The function of ritual is widely misunderstood. Ritual is not magic nor is it merely a psychological tool. Psychologically, when we perform a ritual act we are indeed adding meaning to an otherwise ordinary motion, but we are actually doing much more. Recall the theme of Chapter Two: the Infinite Creator is by definition absolute reality and this world is somewhat illusory. The simplest metaphor to illustrate this theme is the difference between the light of a movie projector and the image on the screen. When we watch a movie, what are we actually seeing? There is a bulb which emits a light, which passes through a film, reflects off a screen and reaches our eyes. The film produces dark patches

1. *Berachos* 15a; *Sukkos* 26b; cf. Rashba and Rosh there.
2. *Shulchan Aruch Orach Chaim* 92:4, 5 and *Mishna Berura* 13. Also before and after marital relations; some also wash ritually after relieving themselves. See also *Mishna Berura* 92:25; *Pri Megadim* 92:4; *Shulchan Aruch Orach Chaim* 233:2; *Tur* 92.

which trick our eyes into thinking that we are viewing real images; in fact, we see only one light.

In this analogy, the light is the Infinite – an infinite light. The images we "see" are the material world around us. We become engrossed in the movie and believe it is quite real – which it is, but not in the way it seems. These multiple things (images) do not really exist – they are illusions produced by the selective filtering of the single light.

If the Infinite Light is the ultimate reality, then actions that are confined to the finite world are ultimately unreal. The only events in this world that are real are those which somehow transcend the finite world and connect to or reveal the Infinite Reality. Therefore when one properly performs a spiritual action, the person, action, and object are all literally transformed from unreal to real – assuming one has the right mental focus.[3]

Therefore a transcendental ritual such as washing the hands has the potential to be an action of utmost creativity, transforming the illusory to the real. The details of this ritual, like much of our meditative tradition, are based on practices in the *Beis Ha-Mikdash* (the Temple). Hand washing recalls the *kohanim* (priests) preparing for their service. But washing the hands is not simply a commemoration. Even while the Beis HaMikdash stood, Jews washed their hands upon rising, before a meal, when leaving a cemetery, etc. The public Beis HaMikdash and its service have always served as a model for the individual path.

3. In *Devarim* 4:29 the verb changes from plural (*bikashtem*, "you sought") to singular (*matzasa*, "you found" and *sidresheinu*, "you will search"), which the Vilna Gaon interprets thus: Only those individuals who "will search" will find; i.e., not all spiritual seekers succeed, only those with the appropriate mental focus. See *Rosh Hashana* 18a.

EXERCISE

Try the hand-washing ritual with kavana upon rising for one week.

1. Fill a large, smooth-rimmed container with water.
2. Make sure the hands are visibly clean.
3. Consider the fact that you are in transition from material to spiritual awareness.
4. Pour water alternately over right and left hands, three times each. Each pouring should cover the fingers completely and most of the hand (ideally to the wrist).
5. Dry hands well.

After one week, try the hand washing at other times of the day, such as before davening (prayer); do it slowly and with kavana.

❧ Focusing the Mind – Contemplation

Each category of pleasure requires a specific type of mental effort, born out of the pleasure itself. For instance, aesthetic pleasure requires that one pay attention to the desired sensory experience. When the mind wanders, it experiences no pleasure from the immediate experience. Consider the game of basketball: the physical and mental exertion can be a great pleasure; yet when a player becomes distracted by pain, worries, thoughts of a loved one or any other thoughts, the enjoyment of the game itself decreases. Moreover the level of play will be diminished, further lowering the pleasure. Pleasure depends, therefore, on focus. This observation reveals why people seek new and exhilarating experiences. Our minds have become so dulled that we need situations of novelty, danger and excitement to derive the same attentive pleasure that a child finds in a leaf or an ant.

Alternatively, we can develop the mind's ability to focus. The simplest method is to practice focusing on an external object.

EXERCISE

Practice Contemplation

Choose a natural object such as a flower or a leaf (an artifact like a pen or a cup will work, if necessary). Choose a time and place where you can sit without interruption. For five minutes, intently examine the object. Study it: notice its colors, shape, texture, smell and taste. Consider its form and function – how do they correspond? How do they correlate?

Finally, hold the object at arm's length and contemplate it as a whole. Where did it come from? How did it get from there to your hand?

Proper contemplation leads to a deeper appreciation of the object. Over time, the practice leads the mind to seek the source of the object – first the physical and then the metaphysical sources. Eventually, the five-minute meditation should result in the mind being in active pursuit of Hashem.

The practice of contemplation resembles learning to play a musical instrument. Imagine a novice who wants to play the piano. She never before touched a piano, but she heard a piece by Chopin and wants to play it, so she sits down at the piano. What will happen? Well, unless she is a prodigy not much is going to happen. She must start with one note at a time and practice consistently to develop skill. Eventually, with discipline and perseverance, most people could probably play Chopin – *if they put their minds to it.*

> A fool sees not the same tree that a wise man sees.
> – William Blake

Contemplation is an exercise to help you develop the mind's ability to focus on something. Most people find that it is not easy to focus for five minutes on one thing exclusively.

47

EXERCISE

1. Choose a time and place to practice a daily contemplation-meditation. Do it for a week. After the first week, do exercise No. 2.
2. Contemplation-meditation is called *hisbonenus*, which literally means "building oneself." Based on your experience doing hisbonenus, explain the relationship between contemplating external objects and self-development.

✦ Developing Constant Kavana

In the long term, hisbonenus develops a mind that can focus at will in various settings. This is the most basic mental skill and the secret to success in many human endeavors, such as:

- speed reading
- musical proficiency
- an athlete's "mental game"
- play (recreation)
- sleep.

As we discussed in Chapter One, focused attention is called kavana. It comes from the root (letters) *kaf-vav-nun,* which means directness or correctness, and the same root is found in the Hebrew words for *to intend, to prepare, be ready* and *to correct.* Rabbi Samson Raphael Hirsch links these words to the two-letter root *kuf-nun,* or *kein* – "yes", suggesting that *kavana* has something to do with affirmation.[4]

The following exercises will enhance your skill of kavana. Enhanced general kavana naturally leads to greater kavana in life situations such as those listed above. It will also greatly assist you in later lessons of this book. The development of kavana clearly involves

---

4. See Hirsch's comment to *Shemos* 2:14.

a shift of perspective as one moves from automatic pilot toward greater awareness and active control. Taking steps to cause such a shift is what is known as becoming a more spiritual person.

EXERCISES

Awareness Enhancement

1. *Develop self-awareness*: Make a list of five actions that you do every day and start a daily record of your level of kavana in each action, on a scale of 1–10. Keep this record for one week.

2. *Develop sense-awareness*: Make five columns or lists, one for each of the five senses, and notice one new thing per day for each sense. Pay attention to colors, smells and shapes. Appreciate the details of the world around you. Keep this record for one week.

3. *Develop habit-awareness*: Become aware of doing an action by rote, such as placing money into your pocket. Why this pocket and not the other one? Why take this route and not another? Take notice of a routine action you perform and bring awareness to it. For example, while brushing your teeth, notice each action and sensation – the weight of the toothbrush, the texture of the bristles, the feeling when you squeeze the paste, the sound of the water.

4. *Catch yourself switching to automatic pilot*: Notice when you turn unaware, begin daydreaming or fidgeting. If you want to daydream, then make a decision to do so, but don't let yourself slip into a dream automatically as soon as you sit down in the metro, set off on a walk, and the like. (This category includes all forms of laziness: lying in bed longer than you need to, watching too much TV, and so on.) Bring awareness to your actions and notice the results.

The goal of Chapter Two was to grasp and internalize the philosophy that Hashem is the Source of everything and in fact is all that really exists, despite our sensory perceptions to the contrary. In Chapter Three, we defined the dual nature of the human being; the tension between our two natures can generate tremendous energy. The key to pleasure in life is to harness that energy.

In this chapter we have developed the foundations of kavana. When we experience the physical world at even the most basic levels of kavana, such as contemplating a leaf, we are transcending our ordinary perception of the world. Transcendence is not someplace in the mind that takes years to discover. It is available immediately with a little effort. Every beginner at contemplative exercises knows that even the initial, unpracticed kavana is vastly richer than that of one who makes no effort.

As the kavana grows with week by week of daily practice, one's awareness should become sharper. The natural result of progress in this area is a mind that is more "present," i.e., aware of the present moment and "the world around me right now."

☙ Deveikus

After beginning to develop the basic mental power of kavana, the next step is to apply this mental skill to the philosophy of Chapter Two, namely, to pursue the constant awareness of God's presence in every place and at every moment.

Such awareness, even when temporary, is called deveikus, which means "connecting" or "attachment" (in modern Hebrew *devek* means glue). To have a constant awareness of Hashem is what it means "to connect" or to attach oneself to God.[5] Hence, the psalmist writes:

> I have set God before me always.
> – *Tehillim* 16:8

---

5. See Ibn Ezra on *Devarim* 10:20 and 11:22, and Ramban there. Alternatively, Rashi there opines that the way to *deveikus* is to spend time with Torah scholars.

This verse has long been understood as a reference to constant awareness.[6]

EXERCISE

In ancient times, *Tehillim* were used for meditation. Some of these meditations concern the act of meditation itself. Consider Psalm 51:12–13:

> *Lev tahor bera-li Elokim*
> *veruach nachon chadesh bekirbi;*
> *Al tashlicheini milfanecha*
> *veruach kodshecha al tikach mimeni.*
> A pure heart create for me, Hashem,
> and a spirit of kavana renew within me;
> Don't cast me away from before You.
> and the spirit of Your transcendence (holiness) don't take from me.

What is the Psalmist saying about kavana and deveikus?

---

6. See Rashi, Ibn Ezra and Meztuda on *Tehillim* 16:8.

Chapter 5

Appreciation

The Art of Saying a Beracha

- ❧ *How Infinite and Finite Coexist*
- ❧ *How to Eat a Piece of Fruit*
- ❧ *Constant Appreciation*
- ❧ *Transcendental Kavana*
- ❧ *Using the Voice*
- ❧ *Anatomy of a Beracha*

My soul thirsts for God,
for the living God.
      – *Tehillim*

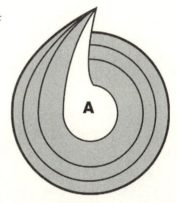

True deveikus or mental and emotional attachment to God does not merely feel right and complete. It is by definition the most real experience one can have in this world. Because deveikus is so wonderful, beautiful and real, it should be a daily goal – not a disconnected, specialized experience, but an awareness of life in all its details.

This deveikus is a specific transcendental level. Ultimately, recalling Chapter Two, the Infinite Creator's essence is unknowable by a finite mind with finite senses. Nonetheless Hashem created this universe for the purpose of giving to another; we are that other and the greatest gift to us is the ability to have a relationship with Hashem Himself. This is a paradox – how can we have a relationship to something that we cannot sense or imagine?

The answer brings us back to the paradox of Chapter Two: at the moment of Bereishis, when the finite world came into being, did Hashem thereby cease to be infinite? After all, now we have an Infinite and a finite which are somehow separate. If so, how can we still call Hashem "infinite"? If this is not so, if Hashem remains totally infinite and not separate from the finite, how is it that we only perceive finiteness around us? In other words, where is the Infinite in relation to the finite?

Another way of asking the question is: From our point of view we understand that the universe was created so many eons ago. But when was it created from Hashem's "perspective," as it were, given that we define Hashem as existing before Bereishis, therefore beyond time? What are the ontological implications of "beginning of time"?

❧ How Infinite and Finite Coexist

Since by definition the Infinite Creator cannot cease to be infinite, from Hashem's "perspective" the universe was created…just now. And now. And now…. At every moment (as we perceive time) Hashem continues to create or cause finite existence. This resolution of the paradox should clarify the meaning of omnipresence – it is inaccurate to describe Hashem as "in everything" (people often say that "God is in me and you"). The diametric opposite is true: Everything is in God. Hashem is the "location" of the universe. Indeed, one of the Hebrew names for God is *Ha-Makom*, "the Place."

In human terms, however, it suffices to understand that

Hashem by definition is always very near to us.[1] This understanding is not intellectually difficult but does require practice to develop into a constant awareness. Judaism seeks to cultivate both an expanded mind and a constant awareness. The practitioner of Jewish "transcendental meditation" seeks to perceive Hashem's manifestation in everything finite and through all of life's experiences.

It is easiest to realize transcendental deveikus when experiencing natural phenomena or during great physical exertion. But we cannot see sunsets every minute of the day, not even once every day. (If we could, we might not need meditation; we could just sit back and...connect.) Life is mundane on the surface, and in order to make that connection and to have that experience of *Wow!* as often as possible we need a meditative discipline.

Sadly, it is in search of this *Wow!* experience that many people have resorted to ingesting chemicals. Some drugs sharpen the senses and enhance the details of life. However, aside from unpleasant side effects, including addiction, these artificial methods are ultimately self-defeating and self-destructive, because they weaken the mind rather than strengthen it. With long-term use, the drugs destroy the very senses they were supposed to enhance. This painful result has been given the apt name burnout.

The path of the Torah works very much in the opposite direction. It is based entirely on the use and development of the mind and the senses. Thus with long-term practice it strengthens the mind significantly. Long-term practitioners report an enviable level of enjoyment of life.

Another benefit of meditative mind-expanders over artificial ones is that meditation is significantly cheaper! It requires neither drugs nor a radical change in lifestyle. It does not require

1. Awareness of this concept is the essence of the verse in the Torah that is known in English as the first of the *Asaras HaDibros* (Ten Commandments, *Shemos* 20:2).

55

any particular personality type. Kavana meditation does require a desire to transcend the mundane. It requires mental and emotional effort. For long-term success, it requires self-discipline. For the beginner, it requires above all an adventurous spirit. The following practice builds on the introductory kavana exercise in the previous chapter.

➤ How to Eat a Piece of Fruit

Find two pieces of the same kind of fruit. Try to choose something fragrant, such as ripe oranges. If it is not orange season, take any fresh, juicy fruit – grapes, pears, watermelon. Before continuing, eat one of the pieces of fruit. It is important not to read ahead until you do this.

Now take the second piece of fruit. Hold it in your hand and notice as many of its features as you can: shape, texture, colors, smell, how it sounds as you manipulate it. It is not necessary to describe it out loud or to enumerate its features. Just notice them. If you run out of features to notice, go back over those you already noticed. Inspect the fruit like a detective. Also, in addition to its finer details, notice the larger features. Notice the fact that it has a protective skin. Notice that its attractive color and smell produce an emotional or even physiological reaction in you.

Now contemplate all that happened in order for this piece of fruit to come into your hand. Many crucial agents were essential for the delivery of this fruit: money bought it; a grocer supplied it; a delivery system brought it to the grocer; a farmer harvested it; a tree produced it; the rain nourished the tree; solar energy brought the rain….

But where did the sun get its energy? While the sun has been shining for a very long time, astronomers and rabbis all agree that it did have an origin. Ultimately, the sun's nuclear fusion – and all energy in the universe – came from the *maaseh Bereishis*. And Bereishis came from the Infinite Creator.

So now we see a direct chain, from Hashem to this fruit in your hand.

Imagine you were sitting on the board of the Ford Foundation, one of the greatest sponsors of scientific research. One day another board member holds up a piece of fruit and declares, "Ladies and gentlemen, this year I want to fund the production of fruits like this in a test tube, from scratch." How much are you going to invest? How much would it cost in research dollars to produce such a fruit from scratch in the laboratory? Millions? Billions?

The answer of course is that it cannot currently be done. No amount of money could create such a technology in the foreseeable future. If it could, the price would be enormous. From this perspective, the orange is essentially priceless. Even one hypothetical day when we might be able to create fruit without seeds and soil, it would be only after astronomical developmental costs. Yet today, with little cost or effort, you are holding one in your hand.

Furthermore, if you pause to think for even a minute, you may realize how strange it is that you are even able to hold such a piece of fruit, that your hand does what you want it to do, that you desire such a piece of fruit, that you have these olfactory glands and taste buds that somehow communicate information to your brain that translates into pleasure....

How did you create the karma[2] to deserve such a precious gift?

As you contemplate the fruit and its history, you should begin to develop a greater appreciation for it. If you contemplate it long enough, your appreciation should develop into joy – joy from the existence of such beauty, joy from thankfulness that you are able to experience such beauty. What an incredible gift!

When you begin to feel joy, eat the fruit. Take your time. Close your eyes. As you chew, concentrate on the taste and texture. Chew slowly. Swallow deliberately.

---

2.   Rambam, *Sefer HaMitzvos*, Mitzva 3; *Sefer Mada* 2:1–2. On "karma" see
     p. 121 note 13.

EXERCISE

Describe the difference between eating the first and second pieces of fruit.

If you did this exercise carefully, including the specific details, you should have gained a deep understanding of the spiritual potential of any aesthetic experience.

According to Judaism, since the Infinite Creator is the source of this universe, He is necessarily the source of every detail of the fruit and of every step of the fruit's production and delivery. Therefore, the ultimate step in basic kavana meditation is to experience the fruit (and all other sensory experiences) with the awareness that the experience is an intimate encounter with HaKadosh Baruch Hu. Recall the principle of the universe as a wavelength of the Infinite Light. When you eat an orange with both appreciation of its details and awareness of its source, you have reached a significant level of transcendence.

To solidify and deepen the connection requires remembering, while contemplating and eating the fruit, that it is a gift. Imagine how you might feel if a dear friend arrived with a personalized gift. Moreover, this particular gift saves your life! For without food, one would literally die: the soul would separate from the body. Food, then, is the primary "glue" that keeps the soul in the body. How can one not think, *What did I do to deserve such beauty*?

By now, many people's appreciation for the fruit becomes so deep that it brings tears to the eyes. If you are such a person, do not fight the tears – let them flow. If you are not so emotional, you are not necessarily lacking; you may be a person who expresses emotions differently. The important thing is to practice focusing on the qualities of your food until the eating experience becomes an emotional experience as well.

❧ Constant Appreciation

Judaism teaches us to take every bite of food with this intense awareness and appreciation.[3] Moreover we should consummate all our sensory experiences with such awareness and appreciation: everything we hear, see, smell, taste and touch. The problem is, for most people it is exceedingly hard to maintain this degree of awareness and appreciation every time one eats.

Similarly, advanced readers sometimes ask, "I've succeeded in enhancing the experience of eating good food, even to the point where the appreciation of the beauty of the gift makes me smile uncontrollably. But how can I have a deveikus experience when I'm eating food that is not so sweet?"

First of all, eat foods that taste good. Avoid bland or bitter foods whenever possible. Second, most of the food we eat has something pleasant about it. It may have a pleasant texture. Or it may be pleasant simply in the fact that it satisfies hunger. So in most cases, we should be able to appreciate something about the food.

But what about bitter pills and medicines? For that matter, what about any painful experience? Is pain an exception to the rule of constant kavana?

Rather than being an exception, pain is also a gift. It can take months or years of contemplation and growth to appreciate pain. For example, I know a man who developed multiple sclerosis at the young age of forty-five. He was a professional musician and music was central to his life, yet the disease made it extremely painful for him to walk, let alone play his instrument. He went into early retirement from his career as a music teacher. At first he was dismayed – would life ever be the same again? Over a period of two years, he learned to play his instrument *with* the pain and despite it, and he told me that the pain taught him to play

---

3. For an idea of the importance of eating in Judaism, consider that the very first commandment in the Torah regards eating (*Bereishis* 2:16) and improper eating is linked to death (*Bereishis* 2:17). For the antidote, see *Yeshayahu* 25:26.

better! And now that he had retired, he had more time than ever before to play.

This man's struggle was not uncommon; his success was. Seekers of higher awareness actually find that the distinction between pain and pleasure diminishes to the point where there is no difference! It is hard to imagine, but that is the goal. This is not a condemnation of pain. On the contrary, Pain is a tool for biofeedback. We can reach a level where we appreciate pain and are thankful for it just as we are for sweet pleasures. It is a gift to help us on our path toward deveikus.[4]

Moreover, pain becomes a greater gift when one has developed kavana as presented in the previous lesson, for pain is usually largely beyond our control. One who has developed kavana will be able to experience pain as a witness as much as a victim. The pain thereby becomes as part of a full life experience.

❧ Transcendental Kavana

The discussion until now has covered the most basic meditative experiences and presented exercises to develop this constant awareness. Hopefully you have been keeping up with these exercises. When one keeps pace, each lesson of this handbook unfolds like a series of doorways leading down a long corridor.

In trying the exercises, you probably came upon a barrier. Most people find it relatively easy to find that momentary *Wow!* even on a daily basis. However, we all find it more difficult to sustain the experience of constant awareness and appreciation for more than a few moments at a time, let alone hours or days.

To illustrate this point, I frequently show an audience a striking photograph of a sunset. In the photo, the light appears to fan outward from the sun in the shape of a light bulb. Once everyone has noticed this unusual feature I explain, "This is a sunset that no one has ever seen. This photo was taken on Mars." Inevitably the room reverberates with appreciative "ooohs" and "mmmms."

---

4. *Nefesh HaChaim*, ch. 1.

Then I ask (with feigned annoyance), "Why do you say "oooh" to this but not to the sound of birds chirping? Or children's laughter? Or to a disposable plastic cup? Or to any of the thousands of astonishing things that we experience every day?"

The answer is obvious: because we have become used to such phenomena. A thoughtful person will agree that the world is full of amazing details – too many! So many that not only would it be impossible to pay attention to all of them, but the very attempt to do so may even be hazardous, such as, for instance, when driving a car or preparing food.

Jewish tradition acknowledges the reality that both extremes are unworkable. One the one hand, total absorption in minuscule details is not practical: our sense of a normal life requires tuning out 99 percent of the information that reaches our senses. On the other hand, to be 100 percent on automatic pilot is the antithesis of the spiritual path.

The middle ground of kavana is one of total focus and appreciation of the beautiful world with which we interact, and acknowledgment of its Infinite Source.[5] The reason that deveikus is so elusive is that the mundane, material world is so obtrusive. We are, after all, creatures of physical habit. We have material needs and desires every day that tend to draw our minds back to the mundane almost as quickly as we try to transcend that mundane. Fortunately, human beings come equipped with several tools that are firmly rooted in the physical world but have a spiritual aspect, thus bridging the gap between mundane and mystical.

One such tool is the mind. The mind's seat in the physical brain allows it to be affected it by material devices such as chemicals. However, the mind is so spiritual that it is exceedingly difficult to control. In order to guide the mind, we use a related, mundane-mystical bridge device, the voice.

5.   Rambam, *Sefer HaMitzvos*, Mitzva 3; *Sefer Mada* 2:1–2.

❧ Using the Voice

The voice employs sounds to concretize that which is happening in the mind, whether intellectual or emotional. While the mind has many physical senses through which it receives information, it expresses its own processes primarily through the voice. The voice turns the mental and mystical into something material.[6]

The Torah frequently refers to the power of words. The process of tuning in to our spiritual selves sensitizes us to this power and we become more careful with our speech. In contrast, we have seen the general decline of word-sensitivity in modern societies. Speech standards have become more and more informal. This decline is unfortunate because it hinders the creation of an environment conducive to spiritual development.

The "power of speech" implies that, although all words are equal, some are "more equal" than others. All words are equal in the sense that any words in any language have a latent transcendental potential. Yet some words are more equal in that some languages seem better suited to make the translation between mystical and mundane.[7]

Hebrew is one such language. According to Jewish tradition, classical Hebrew – *lashon hakodesh* – is the ultimate deveikus language.[8] It was the primordial language spoken by the first person to achieve prophecy, whom the Torah calls "Adam." Hebrew has a poetic purity in which there are no exact synonyms and every sentence has the potential to convey multiple meanings when constructed properly.

Our problem today – indeed, of the past 2,400 years – is that we have lost the ability to tap the full potential of the language. The ancients could achieve great transcendental access by simply

6. *Nefesh HaChaim* 1:13. Technological developments have enabled us to express our thoughts through other media, such as writing, art, music, etc. However, the voice remains the primary, meaning primal, mode of human expression.
7. *See Mishna Berura* 62:3. See also *Mishna Sotah* 7:1 (*Sotah* 32a).
8. See Munk, *The Wisdom in the Hebrew Alphabet* (Mesorah, 1993).

speaking from the heart. That's the power of the Hebrew tongue when used properly. A language is a tool, and Hebrew is like a key to unlock the doors of deveikus – if one knows how to use it.

General knowledge of Hebrew declined in the fifth and fourth centuries B.C.E., during and after the *galus shel Bavel*. In response, the Knesses HaGedola (Sanhedrin) took historic steps to make user-friendly transcendental paths available to the general populace. They composed a series of Hebrew word-combinations which would be less personal than a spontaneous meditation, but which would allow future generations to access the power of lashon hakodesh and to use it for what I have been calling meditation. These word-combinations are called "berachos," a word which at its root refers to a source or a spring.[9]

Readers will recognize the word beracha and even the wording of many of the berachos that follow. If you find yourself thinking, "Aha, now he's talking about blessings" – slow down.

I'm not sure what a blessing is, but I am sure that our understanding of berachos has become as distorted as our conception of "God." Try to avoid the pitfall of applying your prior experience with berachos to the art of kavana. Can you recall the radical difference between eating the two pieces of fruit? There should be a similar radical difference between the way you used to think of a beracha and what you are learning now.

The dilution of Judaism over time has left us a warped understanding of beracha. We would best scrap our pre conceptions and begin here from scratch. Do so, and you will find a radically new Judaism and a real gateway to spirituality.

---

9. Rashi, *Sotah* 10a ("Bameh birchu") states: "Every beracha in the Torah denotes increase, something that causes increase and by which fulfillment is found"; cf. Rabbi David ben R. Yosef Abudarham, *Abudarham Hashalem* (Jerusalem: Even Israel, 1955), vol 1, p. 33. Cf. *Koheles* 2:6. Hirsch understands the essence of beracha to be the concept of spurring new growth, which is exactly the function of a source (comment to *Gen.* 2:3, 9:27, 14:19).

❧ Anatomy of a Beracha

Berachos are tools to achieve deveikus. They are not deveikus it-self. Like all meditative practices, they do not work by magic. A person who utters them casually will gain little,[10] but when said with understanding and kavana, they become a daily source of transcendental kavana, or deveikus.[11]

The beracha thereby resolves our dilemma of how to sustain the transcendental experience; how to walk through life in total deveikus. We may not achieve that level of kavana all day long, but we can certainly reach it whenever we eat. In the parlance of Rabbi Chaim Volozhin, just as food helps the soul connect to the body (because without food, the soul will eventually separate from the body), berachos connect the soul to God.[12]

Ideally, we should all compose our own berachos as needed, and such was the practice in early Jewish history. However, the social-political decline that led to the Babylonian conquest par-alleled a spiritual decline. This spiritual decay was characterized by, among other things, a loss of sensitivity to the language. The Knesses HaGedola therefore codified the berachos in order to

---

10. Rabbi Menachem Lunzano, reprint of *Derech Chayim*, pp 96–100. Cf. Rabbi Yosef Yuzpa Kashman, *Noheg Katzonei Yosef*, as quoted in Mayer Birnbaum, *Pathway to Prayer*, p. 69.

11. While directing the mind and heart to the Infinite Source of the experi-ence, we avoid suggestions that Hashem has parts, and in fact the unity of Hashem is forever beyond our grasp. Rather, we acknowledge that Hashem is the source of this finite experience. That knowledge, followed by sincere emotions of appreciation, can bring one to an extremely high level of deveikus, according to Ramban's definition (see end of ch. 4).

12. *Nefesh HaChaim*, "Eitz Chaim" 62. See also *Nefesh HaChaim* 1:13, where he identifies the mouth as the physiological locus of body-soul fusion. This view explains why we are built in a way that food enters and speech exits at the same locus: food because it maintains the fusion, and speech because berachos maintain the soul's connection to the Infinite; without berachos we are cut off from the Source. Hence, proper use of the mouth is crucial to transcendence.

perpetuate them[13]. Today it is considered improper to compose one's own beracha, both because of our general insensitivity to the nuances of the Hebrew language and because we still need common texts to help preserve Jewish unity.

Although one might think that a standardized text limits creativity, in fact it can be a vehicle for greater creativity. Consider each beracha like a classical sonata. Each of us is a musician, and the creative possibilities are as numerous as the number of musicians. Like music, berachos should be vocalized, not confined to the imagination. Music is the purest expression of emotion and great music can profoundly affect the emotions. Similarly speech is the concretization of thought; hence one can control thoughts via speech. A beracha is a prophetic sound bite that (for most people) must be vocalized to be effective as a meditation.

Most berachos follow the same general pattern:

First, they begin with words that convey the idea of opening a transcendental connection: "*Boruch Atoh/Baruch Ata…*" Baruch is related to the word beracha, and it indicates the source of this moment's life experience. *Atoh/Ata* means "you" – a very personal, endearing appellation for the Infinite Creator! So the berachos begin, in translation, "You are the Source…"

We use the second person because we humans tend to be drawn to those who are familiar to us. Someone to whom I refer as "you" is immediately closer to me than someone to whom I refer as "he." Therefore, although we're talking *about* Hashem and not having a conversation, the Sages gave us berachos in the language that people speak to one another. The meditation is thereby real and personal.

Next, most berachos continue with four names, each of which is an attempt to grasp Hashem within the limits of the human mind. The four words move the speaker from the most obvious to the most sublime:

13. As explained above.

ADONOI/ADONAI	– the Infinite Creator: Who was, is and will ever be
ELOHEINU	– the source of our power (in the natural world)[14]
MELECH	– director, pulling the metaphorical puppet strings
HA-OLOM/OLAM	– the finite world, "concealing" the Infinite

All together, in brief, the typical beracha begins:

You are the Source – the Infinite Creator: Who was, is and will ever be – our power, director of the concealment…

The remainder of the beracha specifies the experience at hand. If the experience is eating a piece of fruit, then the beracha ends with "…creating fruit." Indeed, the four appellations listed above describe a force that surely does create fruit and everything else in life.

Altogether, the beracha is a meditative phrase that aids us in focusing on that piece of fruit and appreciating every aspect of it, including the fact that it exists at all and that I am able to enjoy it!

It is crucial to avoid the misconception that the fruit is infinite, or worse, that the fruit is *the* Infinite. More accurately – to the extent that our language will allow – the fruit is *of* the Infinite. Hashem is there, but then again, He's everywhere. We can choose to eat the fruit in a way that will help us expand our awareness of Hashem's infiniteness. The beracha is thereby a very useful tool to steer our normal perception toward a transcendental one.

Since each beracha addresses a single, isolated experience, in order to infuse one's entire life with kavana, one should try to use berachos in conjunction with the full range of life experiences. This is in fact exactly what the Sanhedrin codified. They wrote berachos for many kinds of experiences that are conducive to capturing a *Wow!* in order to use those moments to transcend

---

14. *Nefesh HaChaim* 1:2–3.

the finite. Their goal was to give the individual a tool to make daily mundane events into mystical experiences.

The Knesses HaGedola included Israel's wisest Sages, among them the three Biblical prophets, Haggai, Zecharia and Malachi.[15] With profound insight into both human nature and lashon ha-kodesh, they created berachos to be used when awaking and when retiring, when eating and when relieving, when putting on shoes and when greeting a long-lost friend, when witnessing natural phenomena, when giving birth and when encountering death.[16]

For instance, there are different berachos for various food types. There is a special beracha for seeing lightning and another for hearing thunder. There is a beracha for seeing a rainbow. There is a special beracha for a parent holding a newborn baby for the first time. There is a special beracha for seeing an unusually beautiful person or animal. There is another beracha for seeing an unusually ugly, deformed creature (which comes from the same source, after all[17]). There is a beracha for unusually good news, and a different beracha for unusually bad news.[18] There is a special beracha for seeing a world-class secular scholar (*"Wow – Stephen Hawking!"*) and even a special beracha for going to the bathroom (*"I can hold it in, and I can let it out – amazing!"*)

> When God has given you a large amount of possessions, do not forget to be thankful for even the minor items…given you.
> – Rabbi Moshe Feinstein

Berachos are so beneficial to expanding one's consciousness that the Talmud recommends saying 100 per day.[19] Divide a typical 16-hour day by 100 and the result is, on average, a beracha every

15. *Sotah* 48b.
16. *Berachos* 33a.
17. *Ibid.* 60b.
18. *Ibid.* 54a.
19. *Menachos* 43b.

ten minutes. Although practically speaking it is easier to cluster them together at certain times throughout the day, the overall effect of striving for 100 is to pepper the day with the kind of meditative moments of appreciation that berachos so successfully create.

The Knesses HaGedola had a secondary goal as well. The Babylonian conquest seventy years earlier had scattered Jews to several parts of the world where they adopted new mother tongues. This demographic dispersion has persisted for 2,400 years. To this day only a minority of Jews live in Israel and speak Hebrew (which has evolved linguistically from biblical Hebrew enough to call it a different tongue). As a counterforce, the canonization of a common liturgy had the effect of maintaining Jewish spiritual unity despite the geographic and cultural dispersion.

The primary building block of that common spirituality is the beracha, which answers the challenge of materialism. The material world presents us with two choices. First, we must choose every day and every moment whether to enjoy it as a gourmet (spiritually) or as a glutton (materially). Second, we choose whether to enjoy it only in itself, or to use the aesthetic experience to leap toward transcendental awareness. The beracha is a user-friendly method for elevating the aesthetic experience into the *wow!* that it should be.

EXERCISES

1. Choose one beracha from the following list and say it with kavana once a day for a week.
2. Learn one new beracha every week and use it with kavana whenever appropriate. Continue to the next lesson after you've learned and used at least four berachos to your satisfaction.

Each beracha begins with:
Boruch ato Adoh-noi (Baruch ata Adonai) Eloheinu melech ha-ohlom
"You are the source – the Infinite Creator Who was, is and will ever be – our power in nature, director of the concealment..."

EVENT	BERACHA
* Hearing thunder	*sheh koh-choh u'g'vuro-soh mo-lei ohlom* (...whose power and might fill the world.)
* Seeing or experiencing an • earthquake, tornado • lightning, comet snow-capped mountain	*...osei ma'aseh vereishis* (continually doing the original action of creation *ex nihilo*).
* Hearing exceptionally • good news shared by two or more people	*...ha-tov v'ha meitiv* (the good and the doer of good).

• bad news (customarily said only on the death of a parent, God forbid)	...*da-yon ho-emes* (the true Judge).
* Seeing the ocean after 30 days or more	...*sheh oh-soh es ha-yohm ha-goh-dol* (making the great sea).
* Eating fruit	...*borei pri ho-eitz* (creating the fruit of the tree).
• or vegetable	...*borei pri ho-adomo* (creating the fruit of the ground).
* Drinking wine or grape juice	...*borei pree ha-gohfen* (creating the fruit of the vine).
* Drinking most beverages or eating animal products	...*sheh-ha-kohl nih-yeh bi-d'voh-ro* (that everything comes from His essence).
* Seeing exceptionally • beautiful trees • or creatures	...*sheh-koh-choh lo b'o-loh-mo* (that even *this* is in His world).
* Seeing an exceptional Torah scholar	...*she choh-lak mei-chohch-moh-so liy-rei-ohv* (who shared some of His wisdom with those who revere Him).
* Seeing an exceptionally deformed person	...*mishaneh ha-brios* (Who varies the creatures).

* Seeing an exceptional secular scholar	*... sheh noson mei-chochmaso levosor vodom* (Who gave of His wisdom to flesh and blood).

* a new
  • house
  • furniture, clothes
  • fruit for the first time this season or seeing a loved one after 30 days of no communication
	...sheh-heh-cheh-yoh-nu, v'kee-y'moh-nu, v'hi-gee-yoh-nu la-z'man ha-zeh (Who kept us alive, and sustained us, and brought us to this season).

Notice that the tag-line of every beracha is expressed in the present tense. This detail helps us be mindful of the concept that for a finite world to exist it must be continually "made" or sustained by its Infinite Source. From our perspective, the universe may be billions of years old, but from an Infinite "perspective" (whatever that may mean, exactly), the universe was created right now. And now! And now...[20].

---

20. See *Likutei Amarim Tanya*, "*Sha'ar HaYichud*" ch. 2.

Chapter 6

Love and Unity

The Art of the Shema

- ➤ *Become a Love Connoisseur*
- ➤ *Mature Love*
- ➤ *Level 1: Transcendental Love*
- ➤ *Level 2: The Unity Meditation*
- ➤ *Level 3: Meditation on Love*
- ➤ *Level 4: The Day of Unity*
- ➤ *Love and Intimacy*

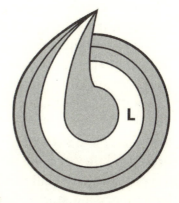

Even when one succeeds in enjoying aesthetic pleasure with total kavana and deveikus, aesthetics cannot hold a candle to the pleasure of loving, caring relationships. Yet how many people are searching for love but cannot define what it is they are looking for? What is love?

Intuitively, most people agree that love is "higher" than sensual pleasure in the sense that one would theoretically forgo any sensory pleasure for the sake of love. Who would forsake true love for any amount of aesthetics?

Imagine, for instance, a stranger who comes to your door with the following offer: "I'll give you fifty million dollars for your daughter. Nothing will happen to her. She'll just move to another country and you'll never see or hear from her again. You won't even get a letter. You won't know a thing about her. But you'll get fifty million dollars." Who would seriously accept such an offer? Fifty million dollars (a mind-boggling amount of sensory pleasure) will not induce you to sell one child. There is no exchange rate; the pleasure of loving relationships is not negotiable for any amount of money.

Now, those parents who just turned down fifty million dollars in exchange for one of their children, what will they do when they walk back into their house and see their kid? They'll run over to her, hug and kiss her, play with her, and say to themselves, "What is this creature that's worth more than all that money? Let's get to know this treasure we have."

If the parents work outside the home, they may realize that while they are practically killing themselves to earn money, they have a fortune at home worth more than they will ever earn, and they are not spending enough time with her. They are so moved that they immediately decide to take that two-week vacation the firm owes them in order to spend time with their riches (i.e., children), and they give the nanny a holiday.

The holiday begins well. They take the kids to the park, read them a few stories, buy them a soda.... The first two hours, they're having a great time. After a little while, things start to get tedious. The kids go from bickering to cranky to aggravating. Dinner is a disaster, giving them baths almost destroys the hallway carpet, and bedtime seems like World War III. Finally at 10:00 P.M. the parents flop down on the couch, turn to each other and say, "Do you really think it was the most responsible thing for us to have taken this two-week vacation? We're both so busy at work, maybe the right thing to do is to go back to work tomorrow morning."

What are these parents missing?

They are not connoisseurs. They never learned what love is and how to get the pleasure of loving relationships. You can play with your kids only so long. Just as we need a course in wine tasting, art appreciation, or anything else to enjoy material pleasures, we need a course in human being "tasting," or appreciation, to maximize our relationships.

❧ Become a Love Connoisseur

There are four steps to becoming a connoisseur of love:

1. UNDERSTAND WHAT LOVE IS.

Love is the emotional pleasure that comes from recognizing another person's inner goodness. Everyone has some amount of goodness in him, but it is often challenging for us to focus on his goodness and not his faults. It is equally challenging to look beyond surface appearances and recognize the personality inside. It is also difficult to focus on who a person is rather than what he does for me. To the extent that one can focus on virtues, one will love others – even if those others are throwing food at each other. One can love them and discipline them at the same time.

This definition of love accounts for how it is possible for people to "love" their cars or other objects. It simply requires focusing on the object's virtues. Since objects, unlike people, have no inner spiritual reality, such love is by comparison ridiculously shallow.

2. OUT WITH THE NEGATIVE.

Since the pleasure called love is a result of mental focus, it can be cultivated. As with many meditative practices, cultivating love requires that you first clear your mind of negative thoughts and then direct your mind toward the object of meditation. The Torah teaches exactly what kind of mental discipline or meditation is required to prepare us to love someone. Judaism considers the famous *passuk*, "Love your neighbor as yourself," a positive precept.

But how can we be obliged to love? The beginning of the verse in *Vayikra* may contain the key:

> Don't take revenge; don't bear a grudge...love
> your neighbor as yourself...(19:18).

In other words, by banishing hostile thoughts and cleansing the mind of negative emotions toward an individual, we can focus on his positive qualities.

This truth is demonstrable by its converse. Without understanding what love is and how to develop it, it is too easy to focus on the effort and pain involved in maintaining a relationship such as marriage or raising children. Sadly, many conclude that these pleasures are not worth the effort.

Every human being is a mixed bag of strengths and weaknesses. Focus on another person's virtues and you will come to love him; focus on his shortcomings and you won't want to spend five minutes with him. The effort of loving is not simply in finding virtues. The real effort is in making a commitment and taking the responsibility *to focus* on virtues and not shortcomings.

3. AVOID "COUNTERFEIT" LOVE.

While the soul seeks love, the body seeks love's counterfeit, infatuation or lust. Today infatuation often passes for love due to the influence of Hellenism, which has competed ideologically with Judaism for 2,300 years. Hellenism expresses its concept of love as an effortless, magical, mystical happening via the figure of Cupid: two people are alone in Central Park, walking under the full moon, and Cupid sneaks up behind them. While he's looking at her and she's looking at him, Cupid shoots them both with an arrow, and they fall hopelessly in love. Effort-free love! However, just as easily as Cupid-love comes, so it departs. Hollywood likes a happy ending so we rarely see the long-term outcome of the romance. What ultimately happens to the couple in Central Park?

They fall in love and get married. Eventually they have kids, a big house, a heavy mortgage…. The husband has to work hard to pay the bills, so he stays overtime at the office. Late one night, while he's working with his secretary, Cupid sneaks up and shoots him again. Now he's in love with his secretary. He comes back to his wife and says, "What can I do, honey, that bum shot me again! I fell in love with the secretary." Out goes the wife, in comes the secretary. That's love, Greek style: not something you can choose but something that victimizes you, something you "fall into."

According to the Greeks, the only way to stay married is to hope Cupid will not shoot again.

Effort-free love is what we call infatuation. As with all material sensory pleasures, infatuation is ultimately not real because it is rooted in the body's desires and will ultimately disappear along with the body. Real love, as all real pleasure, is forever. The way to identify infatuation is to ask: does this feeling come from knowing his or her depth (a spiritual attraction), or does it come from looking at him or her (a physical attraction)? The mind must distinguish between messages from the soul and those from the body. Understand that real love takes real time and therefore real commitment. Infatuation is not love, only sensory attraction.

4. ACCEPT THE REAL PRICE OF LOVE.

Imagine the following scene: Parents come home one day, gather their children around the dining room table and announce that they have fallen in love with the neighbors' children. "Please pack your belongings as they will be moving in tomorrow." Could it happen?

While our children are accidents of birth, we choose our spouse. Therefore, we should expect to see fewer breakups between spouses (or "significant others") than between parents and children. In fact, people rarely disown their children (as tempting as it may sometimes be), yet many divorce their spouses. Why is that? Given that spouses and children can aggravate us equally, how come we do not seriously think of disowning our kids?

Often when teaching about love, I will ask a visibly expectant mother if she will love her child. They invariably respond, "Of course."

"But," I protest, "How do you know your kid will not turn out to be a brat?"

They reply, "I don't know, but I will love him or her anyway." Parents-to-be never say, "Well, we'll have the kid, get to know him, and we'll decide, based on his personality, if we want to keep him or not." How can they be so sure that they will love him?

People know that, as parents, they will be naturally committed to their offspring and appreciate their virtues. We do not fall out of love with anyone to whom we are committed. Thus, parents can claim with confidence that they will love their children despite all shortcomings.

Love between consenting adults, however, is not natural and only comes through effort. The basic effort required is to focus on virtue. Thus, the intensity of love is proportional to the extent to which one appreciates virtues. To know another's virtues in depth takes time, perhaps a lifetime. Therefore, the real price of love is long-term *commitment*. A short-term relationship will deliver relatively limited knowledge and therefore limited pleasure.

EXERCISES

Are you a connoisseur of love?

How do you know whether you are in love or infatuated? If you ever catch yourself saying, "He or she is just perfect," beware! There is no such animal. That's a sure sign of infatuation, not love.

1. Make a mental list of five people whom you love. Ask yourself about each person *Is s/he perfect?* Real love takes work. If we want that pleasure, it's available within every relationship we have if we are willing to make the effort.

2. Think of one person whom you would like to love with real love and commit to making the effort.

● Mature Love

The process of cultivating love leads naturally to a mature loving relationship, which is characterized by a feeling of oneness with an "other." We have all observed older couples who have been together for decades. Not only can they often complete each other's sentences, they even start to look alike. They are becoming one.

We learn this marriage ideal from the story of Adam and Chava. *Bereishis* tells two contradictory versions of their creation:

> VERSION 1 – ...*male and female He created them* (1:27).
> VERSION 2 – ...*and He took one of his sides and closed the flesh in its place. And...built the side that He took from the Adam into a woman and brought her to the Adam* (2:21–22).

What is the official story? Were Adam and Chava created simultaneously as the first version implies, or was Eve formed from Adam? According to the classical reconciliation of the two passages, the original Adam began as a bi-gender being who was then split into two halves. Not only does this interpretation underscore the inherent equality of men and women,[1] it supports the Kabbalistic teaching that before birth, a soul is split into two, one going into a woman's body and the other into a man's. When the two find each other, the experience can literally be the joining of two halves into a new whole.[2]

This definition of love is alluded to in gematria. It is instructive to note that the Hebrew words for love, *ahava*, and for oneness, *echad*, each has a numerical value of 13, hinting at an affiliation between the two.[3] Now we can better understand a mother's natural love for her own children, even before birth. The

---

1. See Hirsch commentary to Gen.
2. Cf. Rashi, (*ibid.*) who observes that a child is literally a new whole produced from equal halves of the parents.
3. See *Kli Yakar* on *Bereishis* 2:5, "*Bayom.*"

child is quite literally an extension of the parent, and the parent therefore feels a sense of unity with the child, regardless of the child's actions.

Similarly, this mature definition of love leads to a recipe for cultivating love: if I want to love someone, I need only to recognize and internalize what we have in common – our common humanity, our common history, our common culture, and so on. My love for any person will grow the more that I can focus on that person's connection to me.

❧ Level 1 – Transcendental Love

As with aesthetic pleasures, the pleasure of a loving relationship can become a transcendental experience with one addition: kavana. When contemplating a loved one, we should not only enjoy the relationship but also think, "This person in my life is an amazing gift!" Through that appreciative kavana, any loving relationship can theoretically become explosively transcendental. The key is to train ourselves to remember every day how everything – including this relationship – is a gift.

❧ Level 2 – the Unity Meditation

We tend to lump all spiritual speech under the heading of "prayer." Prayer means specifically to petition, to ask for something, to request fulfillment of needs and desires. Hebrew has no special word for prayer in the sense of "beseeching God." The closest word to prayer in the strictnse of the term is *bakasha*, "request."[4]

Judaism has another method of spiritual speech that is wrongly associated with Eastern religions – so much so that, like karma, there is no native English word for it, so we use the borrowed Sanskrit word, mantra. A mantra is literally an "instrument of thought" – a word or phrase repeated many times in order to center or guide the mind. One may adopt a mantra and repeat it

4. See Rashi on *Bamidbar* 31:8, where he distinguishes between "tefilla" and "bakasha."

often, in order to unglue the mind from passing thoughts and desires and to guide it toward the desired spiritual goal of transcendence. The mantra is a useful, even powerful, tool to discipline
the mind. But it is not technically a "prayer".[5]

Judaism has both prayers and mantras. We see explicit examples in Tanach of Jews who pray in the tstrict sense.[6] We also
see examples in Kabbala of the use of mantra-like meditations.
These two Jewish spiritual practices have been well documented
elsewhere.[7]

What is less understood about Judaism is its middle path. The
middle path is a meditative practice that was common to all Jews
about 150 years ago, when the Jewish people began to fragment as
never before. The minority who maintain this practice daily find
it powerful enough to develop the most sublime deveikus.

It is called *Krias Shema*, or *Shema* for short. Although it
looks suspiciously like the familiar "Shema Yisrael" that many
Jews learn as children, by the end of this discussion it should look
very different.

THE JEWISH MISSION STATEMENT

Every organization has a mission statement. Skillful managers
know that the success of an organization depends largely on the
degree to which its members have internalized the mission statement. Highly competitive organizations find creative ways to remind their members of the mission.

The Shema meditationis the Jewish people's mission statement. It is written in the Torah[8] and is the simplest and purest

---

5. *Berachos* 31a. See Rashi there, who defines tefilla as "praise." See also the
    Introduction to Rabbi Shimshon Pincus, *Sha'arim BeTefilla* and p. 93.
    While prayer is indeed a form of meditation, its goal is not concentration
    per se.
6. E.g., *Bereishis* 20:17, 25:21, 32:10–13, and *Shemos* 32:11.
7. See Aryeh Kaplan, *Meditation and the Bible*; also *Meditation and Kab-
    bala*.
8. *Devarim* 6:4.

kavana meditation of all time. This single phrase captures the essence of the classical Jew: a transcendental seeker, one who contemplates and struggles to grasp Hashem, a witness to the essential unity of all things and a member of a tribe whose mission it is to preserve and perfect these modes of awareness.[9]

To use the Shema properly requires a study of its nuances. The complete phrase is:

SHEMA YIS-ROH-EIL ADONOI ELOHEINU ADONOI ECHOD.

SHEMA – *hear*, as an imperative, meaning not just hearing but also deep understanding, at the gut level (internalizing)

YIS-ROH-EIL – *the Jewish people*. The root means, "struggles with the Infinite"[10]

ADONOI – *the Infinite Creator*: Who was, is and will ever be

ELOHEINU – *the source of our power in the natural world*[11]

ADONOI – *the Infinite Creator*: Who was, is and will ever be

ECHOD – *one*, meaning absolute one-ness, or perfect unity

---

9. See *Mishna Berura* 62:3, which summarizes the kavana of the Shema as *ikuva*, "essentiality." See *Sefer HaTanya, Sha'ar Hayichud*, ch. 7.

10. *Bereishis* 32:29; this is one of several classic interpretations of "Yisroel" based on the obscure word *sarisa*. The full verse reads: "Your name will no longer be said as Yaakov, rather Yisroel, because you have *sarisa* with God and with men and done well." The word *sarisa* may mean "excelled," "been straight" (as opposed to the "crooked" nature of a "Yaakov" which means bent) or "struggled." Since the context is an all-night wrestling match, many prefer the latter (see Radak there). Cf. *Hoshea* 12:4–5. Alternatively, Rashi, citing *Midrash Rabba*, interprets "Yisroel" as *yashar-Kel*: "the upright of God": i.e., you were once known as "crooked," because you appeared to use trickery, but now you'll be recognized as righteous. Based on Rashi, one says the words "Shema Yisroel" with the self-image of one who is attempting to remain righteous despite adversity. Hirsch points out grammatically that *sarisa* means "you had power;" thus, homiletically, if a lowly person like Yaakov can prevail, then there must be a higher power making it so.

11. See Rashi on *Bereishis* 2:5.

Put together the meditation reads:

SHEMA YISRO-EL

Understand deeply, you who struggle with the Infinite:

ADONOI ELOHEINU;

the Infinite Creator (Who was, is and will ever be) is our power in the natural world;

ADONOI ECHOD.

the Infinite Creator (Who was, is and will ever be) is absolutely one.

How do we use this statement? It is a universal Jewish practice to say the Shema meditation twice every day, morning and evening. This timing is derived from the Torah's phrase, to "speak these words…when you go to bed and when you get up."[12]

Choose a place with minimal distractions. It may be a quiet room or a location outside. Let the other members of your family know not to disturb you for five or ten minutes. If necessary, unplug the phone.

1. PREPARE THE BODY. Wash your hands (review Chapter Four for why and how). Assume the basic meditation position (see the end of Chapter Two, exercise one).
2. PREPARE THE MIND. If you are meditating in the morning, spend a few minutes thinking about light; if it is evening, spend a few moments thinking about the transition from day to night. In either case, follow with a few moments thinking about love.
3. COVER THE EYES WITH THE RIGHT HAND. Think about your goal – a total understanding and internalization of the oneness of Hashem.

12. *Devarim* 6:7.

4. *SAY THE SIX WORDS OF THE SHEMA PHRASE.* Think about the meaning of each word as you say it. Say the words aloud. Hear your voice intone them.

5. *REPEAT AS MANY TIMES AS YOU NEED.* The goal is to say the entire phrase at least once with 100 percent kavana.[13] If you realize, for instance, that upon saying "echod" you did not have kavana on the word *Yisro'el*, say the whole thing again. When you arrive at the "d" of "echod" and feel a total concentrated transcendence, stop repeating the phrase.

6. *WARM-DOWN.* Bring yourself back gently to space-time by whispering the mystical tag-line:

BORUCH SHEIM KEVOD MAL-CHUSO LE-OLOM VO-ED.

The revelation of the awesomeness of Hashem's omnipresent and omnipotent manifestation is the source of blessing for the eternal hidden world.[14]

That's a real mouthful in English and requires an explanation. The word *sheim* in the vernacular means "name," and in the mystical language of classical Hebrew the name of a person or thing reveals that person or thing's essence. Therefore the *"Boruch sheim"* tag-line literally refers to Hashem's four-letter Name, spelled *yud + heh + vav + heh*. This Name expresses as much of Hashem's revealed or manifest essence as is possible in this world.

Consequently this four-letter Name is awesome, and a spiritual seeker should approach it with real humility. Consequently, we have a universal custom not to pronounce it as written. Instead, we pronounce it "Adonoi," having in mind "the Infinite," Who was, is and will always be. This pronunciation, Ah-doh-noi, also has

---

13. Mishneh Torah, *Sefer Ahava, Hilchos Krias Shema* 2:1; *Shulchan Aruch Orach Chaim* 63:4 and *Mishna Berura* there, 12–15. See also Taz on *Orach Chaim* 61:9. However, one should strive to say it right the first time.

14. Cf. Hirsch, et al. *perushim* on *Devarim* 6:4. Others connect "Baruch Sheim" to "Yehei Shmei Raba" of Kaddish (*Targum Yerushalmi*).

the connotation of "Master of the universe" which indicates one aspect of our relationship to God.

Some modern groups have tried to pronounce the four-letter Name as written.[15] This practice is a serious spiritual error, for to do so is akin to flippancy about the manifest essence of God.[16] The universal Jewish practice today is to be so sensitive to the power connected to this Name that in casual speech we are taught to avoid even uttering the ersatz name *Adonoi* (except in the Shema and other prayers), substituting instead *Ha shem* – literally, "the Name."

Now by definition Hashem must be totally manifest in the finite – *He is everywhere, all the time*! In times of need, many people, regardless of religious background, do express some transcendental awareness through prayer and/or meditation. Nevertheless, in ordinary times, most people remain ensconced in nature and naturalism, ignoring the concept of an omnipresent and omnipotent Infinite.

This fact of human nature is why in the Shema we say "*Eloheinu*" – "our" power in nature. From the dawn of Jewish history until today, this knowledge has yet to become universal. Before saying the Shema, remember too that millions of Jews say this "mission statement" twice a day, every day, as we have for thousands of years.

Still, our own knowledge is limited. From the greatest to the smallest, we are all mere seekers of spiritual understanding. True, we may develop our awareness of Hashem's manifestation in the finite world – this is the goal of Judaism's meditative practices. This

15. The most common are the J-Witnesses and the academics. The difference between the two is that the J-Witnesses are using the name *lesheim Shamayim*; the academics have the opposite intention. In recent years, there has been a significant increase of traditional Jews participating in academia, resulting in tension and offense.
16. *Nedarim* 7b. When teaching Jews who do not have the *yiras Shamayim* (awe of Heaven) to appreciate the traditional concept of *aveira*, I explain, truthfully, that this practice "generates dreadful karma."

awareness is awesome – *amazing!* The fact that we can express this awareness is more amazing still.

But there are even greater dimensions of kavana.

In seeking Infinite awareness, Jewish tradition often represents Hashem with the metaphor of a king whose kingdom is Infinity. According to this metaphor, human beings have a greater role than that of being passive recipients of Infinite pleasure. A "king" cannot rule without "subjects." If there were no humans to actively "crown the Infinite king," so to speak, then He could not be king. The Infinite could not have a meaningful or relevant relationship to the finite. In other words, by choosing to receive, we *make it possible* for Hashem to give.

This is an amazing insight and an awesome responsibility, which leads to several startling conclusions. Consider, for instance, the beracha of Chapter Five. At the basic level, the purpose of the beracha is to expand an aesthetic pleasure, such as eating a piece of fruit, into a transcendental deveikus-pleasure. We can now see that something else is happening when we say a beracha with kavana.

Recall that the purpose of this universe is for our total pleasure, the greatest of which would be infinite, transcendental pleasure. In other words, our purpose is to elevate the physical and to make our interaction with it and our experience of it transcendental. That is, to reveal God's manifestation. Therefore, if human beings ceased to use the physical for ultimate (transcendental) pleasure, there would be no ultimate purpose for the existence of that physical pleasure. Hashem would cease to make that physical pleasure manifest. In other words, if people stopped making berachos on oranges, oranges would stop growing.[17]

This awesome responsibility is taught in many places in Jewish tradition, the first of which is the Torah's account of Adam, the first *Homo sapiens,* the first creature with an Infinite soul:

---

17. See *Tosafos, Berachos* 43a.

All the trees of the field were not yet on the earth and all the plant
life of the field not yet sprouted, for Hashem-Elokim had not
caused rain to fall and there was no Adam to work the ground.
    – *Bereishis* 2:5

The *Midrash* explains that the rain started to fall as soon as Adam
asked for it.[18] Now, as Chapter Seven will explain, the Torah is not
a history book; we are meant to ask what this passage can teach
us. To which one might answer that the basic lesson is the interdependent relationship between physical blessings and ourselves.
Not only do we depend on blessings, the blessings depend on us.

> The beracha thus creates a new reality – one in which
> the blessings from the Infinite Creator may descend
> upon the one who has uttered the beracha.
>   – Rabbi Aaron Twerski[19]

We are in fact describing Jewish "karma," mentioned in previous
chapters. The basic principle of karma is that our words and actions in this world have both material and spiritual effects. When
enjoying the material world, since we already have the experience
in our hand (in the case of food, literally in our hand), we cannot
say that this current experience depends on the utterance of a beracha, because it is clearly possible to have the experience without
a beracha. Therefore, if the beracha does have a karmic effect, that
effect must be on future experiences.

Our words, then, can have tremendous power.

This potential of our own words helps clarify the discussion
above, regarding the indirect way we pronounce the four-letter

---

18. *Yerushalmi Taanis* 2: the word *eid* ("mist") in verse 6 can be read as
    "prayer." See Rashi on *Bereishis* 2:5, where he paraphrases Tractate *Chullin*
    60b.
19. "100 Times a Day", in Rabbi Binyamin Forst, *The Laws of B'rachos* (New
    York: Mesorah, 1990), p. 29.

Name. We do not avoid the name altogether. In a beracha, as well as in the Shema, we do meditate on the Name, using the pronunciation AH-DOH-NOI. With deep kavana, these meditations can feel pretty good. In fact, when one says the six-word Shema meditation with kavana, it can feel as though one has grasped the essence of Hashem.

This feeling jibes well with the transcendental reality of God. The transcendental reality should be stop-you-in-your-tracks-speechless, jaw-droppingly awe-inspiring. The four-letter Name, which expresses that reality, should likewise be awesome. This Name has such power that Jewish practice strictly limits pronouncing it to once per year by the high priest in the Jerusalem Temple, to be heard by the assembled public. He utters it after many hours of intense physical and mental preparation and purification on Yom Kippur, the day the entire nation have most intensified their physical and mental purification.

This tradition teaches us a lesson in humility. One should think, "How can I even momentarily think that I truly grasp Hashem's essence?"

Therefore, to hedge our kavana, the BORUCH SHEIM…tagline reminds us that we really cannot properly relate to the name that we are trying to say. The tag solves the dilemma of the Shema meditation: when said with kavana, one can have the feeling of actually grasping the essence of the Name. The tag brings us back down to earth. It reminds us that the energy associated with the Name is really beyond our grasp.

Please review the tag-line and its translation, above. Then try the following exercises.

EXERCISE

1. Try the first-level Shema meditation. Do it for a week, either every morning or every evening, or both morning and evening.
2. After doing the Shema meditation for at least a week, make a commitment to yourself to continue daily for three more weeks.
3. After doing the Shema meditation for a week or two, continue with level three, below.

● Level 3 – The Meditation on Love

By itself, the first line of the Shema is a meditation of awesome power. We can harness that power to tap into the deepest, most beautiful human emotions. While everyone has the capacity for these emotions, they do not always come naturally. It has been observed that the degree to which we feel fondness for someone or something is directly proportional to the amount of time spent on it. We tend to develop fondness for those with whom we spend the most time. This model gives us an alternative explanation as to why people can "love" their cars. The typical car lover does not spend time with his car only because he loves it; he loves it more because he spends time with it!

In other words, love can be cultivated. Contrary to popular belief (and song), love need not be spontaneous. Most of what people experience as "love at first sight" is probably infatuation or lust, i.e., self-centered desire. After all, how could it be true love? True love by definition develops from the appreciation of another person's virtues. This appreciation may take weeks, months, or even years to acquire. A true lover is like a true painter: he will take as much time as needed. Love is indeed an art form – a sophisticated craft that demands creative brilliance and hard work.

Now when we say the short Shema meditation properly, we find that doorways open within us, doorways that lead to our own infinite qualities. The general name for this range of qualities is *love*. Love is the best word we have for that aspect of a human being that is most akin to God. This point is symbolized by the Hebrew words for love, *ahava*, and for oneness, *echad*. Both words have a numerical value of 13, hinting at an affiliation between the two. Combined, 13+13 = 26, which is the numerical value for Hashem's unspeakable Name, *yud, heh, vav, heh*, 10+5+6+5.

Moreover, the three-letter root of *ahava*, *aleph-heh-beis*, has the numerical value of eight. Throughout Torah, eight represents infinity, which is appropriately symbolized by our modern numeral 8 (turned sideways). Therefore, since the gates are open, the logical continuation of the short Shema would be a deeper meditation on infinite love. When we say the Shema well, we should feel so connected that this connection itself takes over our emotions. It activates a powerful urge to connect to that Source of light and love. Our instinctive response is to want more light and love.[20]

This is indeed the next step. The Torah itself teaches a deep meditation on love immediately after the first line of the Shema meditation. Why love? Again, because that is what we should be feeling after saying the Shema. To say the love paragraph with kavana will help us meditate with more kavana in the future, which in turn helps us develop more love...and so on.

20. Refined feelings are the result of spiritual work, not the work itself. Despite our desire for immediate emotional gratification, the mind should lead the heart and not vice-versa. As we improve our understanding of life and of ourselves, our emotions mature naturally (*Nefesh HaChayim*, ch. 13).

EXERCISE

1. Compare and contrast: prayer, mantra, Shema.
2. After taking the time to learn the Shema meditation with proper kavana, begin to use the second paragraph. Start by reading the translation carefully. As always, make sure that you have crystal clarity at each step of the journey.

Follow the same technique outlined above. For the sake of maximum accuracy in pronunciation, follow the transliteration with care. The consonant "ch" (in transliterated Hebrew, sometimes written "kh") is pronounced gutturally and sounds like someone coughing to clear his throat. Say aloud, with eyes closed:[21]

SHEMA YIS-ROH-EIL

Understand deeply – you who struggle with the Infinite

ADONOI ELO-HEI-NU

the Infinite (Who was, is and will ever be) is our power in nature;

ADONOI E-CHOD.

the Infinite (Who was, is and will ever be) is absolutely one.

Now whisper:

BARUCH SHEIM K'VOD MAL-CHU-SO L'O-LOHM VOH-ED.

The revelation of the awesomeness of Hashem's omnipresent and omnipotent manifestation is the source of blessing for the eternal hidden world.

---

21. The translation follows the *perush* of several authorities, including Rashi, Rambam and Ramban. See *Devarim* 6:4–9.

Continue in normal voice:

V'OH-HAV-TOH EIS A-DO-NOI ELLO-HEH-CHOH,
Love the Infinite Creator, your power in nature,

B'CHOL L'VO-VEH-CHOH,
with a full heart (i.e., both spiritual and material drives),

U-V'CHOL NAF-SH-CHOH,
with your entire soul (willing to die for transcendental pleasure),

U-V'CHOL M'O-DEH-CHOH.
and with all your resources (willing even to spend money for transcendence).

V'HOH-YU,
And they will be,

HA-D'VOH-REEM HOH-EI-LEH ASHEIR OH-NO-CHEE
M'TZA-V'CHOH HA-YOM,
these words with which I give you transcendental access today,

AL L'VOH-VEH-CHO
upon your heart (internalized into both spiritual and material drives).

V'SHEE-NAN-TOHM LE-VOH-NEH-CHOH, V'DEE-BAR-TOH
BOHM,
And you will imbue your children with them, and meditate with them

B'SHIV-T-CHOH B'VAY-SEH-CHOH, U'V'LECH-T'CHOH VA-
DEH-RECH,
both sitting at home and traveling on the road,

U-V-SHOHCH-B-CHOH UV-KU-MEH-CHOH.

both in the evening and in the morning.

U-K-SHAR-TOHM L'OHS AL YOH-DEH-CHOCH,

And you'll bind them as a symbol of physical discipline to your arm

V'HOH-YU L'TO-TOH-FOS BEIN EI-NEH-CHOH.

and they'll be a sign of mental discipline between your eyes

U-CH-SAV-TOHM AL M'ZU-ZOS BAY-SEH-CHOH

And you'll write them on the doorposts of your house

U-VI-SH'OH-REH-CHOH.

and on your gates.

DISCUSSION

The theme of the meditation is the constant awareness of Hashem throughout one's daily life, as introduced in Chapter Four. A person who is aware and observant is sometimes called an *eid*, a witness. The first line is written as a testimonial: *Hear and understand…!* As a post-modern twist to an ancient text, in every Torah scroll in the world, from Yemen to San Francisco, two letters in this phrase are written much larger than the rest of the line. These two letters, *ayin* and *daled*, spell *eid* – witness.

The long paragraph above continues this theme of awareness, taking us from pure transcendental awareness through some of the details of the love created through that intimate awareness.

✿ Level 4 – the Day of Unity

The Shema meditation, particularly the first six words, is a tool to re-focus on the true transcendental potential of the world. Paradoxically, in order to tune in to this reality, we tune out certain aspects of the world. For a moment, we tune out life's pressing details. Hunger, work, family, friends, war, peace, telephones, music and television, machines, pencils, dirty laundry, money – all become irrelevant for a moment while we reconnect to something much more lasting and satisfying. Who would not benefit from a daily five-minute meditation like this?

Imagine taking the time every week to live an *entire day* with oneness, literally to turn off and put aside those activities that keep us attached to the mundane side of this world: radios, music and television, appliances, computers, laundry, money, work – a whole day of Shema, of hearing! A day of outward focus, of human relationships, without the pressure to accomplish or to produce; a day of inward meditation to reconnect to ourselves and to something greater. This incredible idea is by itself worth the price of this book: to spend twenty-four hours seeking "infinity in a grain of sand, heaven in a wild flower" (William Blake). A single day spent without seeking to manipulate, only to enjoy life at every level.

Now imagine an entire community practicing such a day of meditation. It is instructive to see Yisrael as a synthesis of East and West. In the stereotypical East, we see cultures dominated by communal focus. The welfare of the community takes precedence over the ambitions of the individual. Social norms and hierarchies are dominant and stable. In the stereotypical West, we see cultures dominated by the individual focus. The rights of the individual take priority over the cohesion of the community. Social norms and hierarchies are fluid and routinely challenged.

The Jewish ideal balances the community and the individual by shifting the concept of individual rights to individual responsibilities. It is a subtle shift that can transform the social relationships that are the foundation of the community. For instance, imagine a society where, instead of the needy competing for limited social welfare, we have many people competing to help the impoverished. If everyone considers it a sacred responsibility to give ten percent of their income to the poor, it would become increasingly difficult to find poverty. Under this ideal, the dominant, inviolate social norm is to give to others. The freedom of the individual is the freedom to choose whether or not to give and how and when to give.

Internalizing this sense of responsibility – balancing East and West – is the key to loving relationships. To develop a culture of such loving responsibility seems, historically, to require a day when economic and social competition ceases and individuals can focus exclusively on their individual meditations and social relationships.

To *be* for a day – to stop changing the world – is the true meaning of Shabbos, a weekly rhythmic interlude of spiritual rest, meditative contemplation and community building.[22] Although many find this orientation attractive, they rationalize, "Maybe I'll try it when I have time…." *Perhaps you'll never have time?*[23]

❧ Love and Intimacy

The stronger the potential love bond, the stronger the potential material quagmire is likely to be. Marriage has fantastic love potential, which is why the drive for intimacy is so strong. When practiced outside of a committed, lifelong relationship, one risks feeding his bodily desire at the expense of his soul's desire for love. Alternatively, in the context of love (i.e., unity), intimacy can deepen that unity-love to the point of inexpressible profundity.[24]

The two challenges of loving relationships should now be evident: how to enjoy them and how to use them as vehicles for

---

22. See Isaac E. Mozeson, *The Word: The Dictionary that Reveals the Hebrew Sources of English*, p. 169.
23. *Avos* 2:17.
24. The transcendental potential of intimacy exists for two reasons. First, the mystical tradition interprets the intimacy between a man and a woman as an analogy to that between the Infinite and the finite. Second, the creation of a child – a new living creature – is the most "Divine" creative activity available to us. This framework is not to negate the possibility of loving intimacy without the potential for procreation. Rather, the point is that the potential for procreation – even the imitation of the potential – adds a transcendental dimension to the intimacy, when practiced with kavana.

amazing spiritual transcendence. The exercises in this chapter should lead toward a love experience so profound that it is hard to imagine a greater pleasure. Nevertheless, there is one pleasure dimension even greater than love, as the next chapter elaborates.

Chapter 7

Being Good

The Art of Mussar

- *The Difference Between Right and Wrong*
- *Morality (Ethics) As a Body-Soul Struggle*
- *Good Isn't Good Enough: A Path to Greatness*
- *Transcendental Goodness*

Everyone wants to do what is right. According to a *U.S. News and World Report* poll, nine of every ten Americans say that they consider themselves good people. Are they right? On what basis do they say so? According to the poll, among this 90%, 80% judge themselves more favorably than Mother Teresa and 70% more favorably than Michael Jordan. The fact that most people judge themselves so favorably indicates a deep psychological phenomenon: Being ethical is so important that few can bear the possibility of being unethical. Not only do we consider ourselves "basically good," but we even tend to think of ourselves as "better than most." According to this poll, most of us consider ourselves saintly. Yet somehow we bristle at the idea that even Hitler, in his own warped way, believed that he was righteous. If Hitler could be so evil yet consider himself good, what about we who are so...?

No, file the Hitlers of the world under the category of crazy rather than use them as an opportunity to introspect and to evaluate our own righteousness.

> I'm a moral person but I think, like most
> people, my moral values are pretty fuzzy.
> – Mick Jagger

A DEFINITION

Good or *ethical* means acting in accordance with an absolute value. For example, in every society most people believe that to murder is wrong, or evil, and not to murder is good; that robbery is evil and honesty is good; etc. If so, why do so many people commit murder, rob, lie, and cheat?

There are two underlying reasons. One reason is the multiple definitions of what, exactly, constitutes murder, robbery, and so forth. Some would say the evil of murder includes the killing of animals. Some say the termination of a pregnancy is murder. Others disagree. A second reason for the prevalence of these evils is that people tend to rationalize: "I know this is wrong, but...." Or: "I know his behavior is bad, but he has a good heart." Normal people simply do not knowingly and intentionally commit or abet evil.

Our aversion to evil is in fact so strong that in order to avoid it we would be willing to sacrifice not only physical pleasures but even loved ones – even life itself. For instance, imagine you were on a plane hijacked by terrorists. They come up to you and say, "Either you kill these three hundred innocent people on the plane – here's the gun, go and slaughter them – or we'll kill your kids." What would you do? Could you kill three hundred innocent people? You couldn't do it. Even though you have five kids you adore, you still could not kill three hundred innocent people. Why not?

Because it's wrong.

The devil's advocate asks, "But wait a minute. Are you some angel? Didn't you ever do anything wrong in your life? What's the big deal? Do one more wrong thing."

"No. It's *too* wrong. It's not worth it."

"What's not worth what?"

"The pleasure of my loving relationships is not worth giving up the pleasure of being good."

Do you realize what you are saying? You are willing to give up your most cherished loving relationships in order to avoid evil and to be ethical. Goodness is a greater or higher type of pleasure. If the example of the three hundred innocent lives doesn't resonate, choose a higher number – three thousand or even three million. At some point, every sane person draws the line and says that he would rather give up a loved one than commit evil.

Now if the pleasure of being good outweighs much of what we have in life, we should learn how to enjoy that pleasure.

Judaism teaches: If you do not know what you're willing to die for, you have not begun to live. If you have no self-respect, no belief that you yourself are a good person, you are not yet living life to the fullest. The drive for self-respect is so strong that most people consider themselves good even if they have never examined what it means to be good.

Contrast this unawareness with our attitude toward the pleasures discussed in previous chapters. People don't mind admitting their lack of physical pleasure; we readily and openly discuss our search for loving relationships (and the transparency of these two unmet needs drives major sectors of our economy). Yet where are all the seekers of righteousness? Part of the problem is a culture that has drummed into us a notion of tolerance so broad as to accept all perspectives and lifestyles as equally good.

☙ The Difference Between Right and Wrong

Although there are a lot of gray areas, I used to take comfort in knowing that there were certain deeds that were universally accepted as good or bad. For instance, everyone in every land agreed that it would be good to save a small child's life and wrong to murder.

Then came 9/11.

On 9/11 we learned about a group of people who, not out of anger or despair but for rational, thoughtful reasons, concluded that it would be good to murder thousands of people.

They didn't even call it murder.

Now 9/11 was not new in this respect. The Jewish people have had small and large 9/11s since the beginning of our history. The 9/11 that occurred on September 11, 2001, was just the most recent episode of "in every generation they will rise to destroy us." In each of these episodes, how do we know we're right and they are wrong? How does a lone iconoclast like Avraham know that it is possible to be right "even if the rest of the world says you're wrong"?[1] What is the proof that we should not all convert to Islam?

First, we know that whatever sense of absolute right and wrong we have is something we believe irrationally. Even the Declaration of Independence resorted to "self-evident" truths. The deepest truths cannot be proven, they can only be revealed. It is likely that every sane human being on earth agrees that killing an innocent person is murder. The disagreements stem from how to define "human" – for instance, Nazis and jihadists may define *person* as "non-Jewish." In other times and places people have defined *human* as "white," "wealthy," and even "male."

When confronted with this apparent chaos of values, the Torah reminds us that our perception of events in this world is fundamentally illusory. There really is only one absolute, true re-

---

1. With no sense of irony, UN Secretary-General Kofi Annan spoke thus of Israel during its military response to such violent assaults.

ality – the Infinite Source of existence. Thus, the Torah defines *good* simply as a belief or activity that interfaces with or is consistent with that Source, whereas *bad* is a belief or activity that does not interface or is inconsistent with that Source. Even more simply put, *good* is that which draws me closer to God (creating greater deveikus) and *bad* or *evil* that which draws me away from that Source.

This streamlined definition of good does not fully resolve the problem. It still leaves room for interpretation of what kinds of beliefs and activities draw one closer to God. Some would claim that the answer is completely subjective. The problem with such a view is that there are some beliefs and activities that most of us label "bad" without hesitation.

For example, a Taliban terrorist may claim that flying an airplane into a building full of civilians would bring him closer and faster to the Infinite Source. Most non-Taliban disagree: it is not merely a subjective choice. Prior to 9/11 such an example would have seemed grossly exaggerated and inappropriate. Unfortunately, our collective karma is forcing us more and more to confront these ethical questions and refine our own moral principles. Perhaps events like 9/11 and the Holocaust have helped clarify in our hearts that there are indeed some beliefs and actions that are evil.

But the struggle is just as real on the individual level. If I am feeling grumpy, is it wrong to act grumpily toward my spouse? Perhaps for the sake of honesty, acting grumpy would be right. Without a framework, it is impossible to answer such a question with any ethical certainty. What we gain from the Torah definition of good is the ability to say that certain actions (and beliefs) are objectively good and others are objectively bad. How to differentiate objectively remains to be seen.

☙ Morality (Ethics) As a Body-Soul Struggle

Let us consider a person who has enough moral clarity to know without any doubt that stealing is wrong – evil, in fact. What might lead such a person to steal?

Consider the scenario of a vice-president of a company who has made a mistake that will cost the company thousands of dollars. The only other person who knows about the mistake is a secretary. What should the manager do – blame and fire the secretary ("It's my word against hers") or admit the mistake: saying effectively, "I'm wrong"? What would motivate an otherwise decent person to blame the secretary? Whether or not telling the truth will result in material consequences, most people have a hard time admitting their mistakes for fear of looking bad. Looking bad – a painful experience for the body – is a powerful disincentive to honesty.

Yet time and time again we hear of people who confess their mistakes, sometimes many years later. For many years they choose to *look* good rather than to *be* good – following the body rather than the soul. Yet all along, the soul clamors for the pleasure of being good, the pleasure of self-respect.

HOW TO LEARN HOW TO BE GOOD

As a child grows, she learns slowly to identify the different forces within her. One voice says, "Hit your brother." The other voice says, "Leave him alone." If *good* refers to actions that draw her closer to the Infinite Source and *bad* to those that draw her away, she can interpret the two voices within the context of the body-soul struggle that makes our spiritual growth possible. Thus, the first voice ("hit your brother") is her body (material self) and the other voice ("leave him alone") is her soul (spiritual self).

In real-life situations, it is easy to tell the difference. Whenever you are contemplating doing something and are not sure if it would be right or wrong, ask yourself the following questions: What do I *feel* like doing? What do I *know* is the right thing to do? In an ethical decision, *what I feel like doing* is always the body talking and *what I know is the right thing to do* is always the soul talking.

EXERCISE

Identify your ethical choices.

Appreciating the pleasure of our own goodness is a level of kavana. In order to develop this appreciation, make a list of ethical choices you have faced today (whether or not you chose well). This is the first step to becoming a connoisseur of anything – learning to discriminate between different qualities.

Place a check mark beside those choices in which you chose to do what you believe is right and an x beside those in which you chose to do what you felt like doing.

Make such a list every evening for one week. The goal is to develop awareness of ethical choices as we are making them.

As a person grows morally, one trains the body (feelings) to conform to the soul (knowledge) so that one's "gut reaction" becomes more and more consistent with the spiritual or good path. The synchronization of body with soul is what we call maturity.

One might suppose that highly mature individuals get their bodies so in tune with their souls that they eventually run out of moral choices. This might be true if the soul were finite. But since the soul is rooted in an Infinite Source, spiritual growth too is infinite. A spiritually mature person indeed faces daily moral choices. The difference between a spiritually immature person and a spiritually mature person is the degree of refinement of those choices.

For instance, most of us at least occasionally struggle to control our impatience with certain people. Every workplace has at least one of them: the obnoxious guy, the rude woman, the conceited person. A highly spiritual individual will not struggle with whether or not to show kindness to such a person but may struggle with whether or not to give that person an extra few minutes of kindliness.

Our history is resplendent with spiritual giants who lived up to such standards. Open any biography of any Jewish sage and one finds story after story of great kindness and generosity extended under the most trying circumstances – circumstances that the average person would not have tolerated. The basic generosity is not an issue for such great people – this is part of their nature. Their moral struggles are over minute details that would be trivial to the rest of us.

To give but one example: HaRav Moshe Feinstein, *zichrono leveracha*, always attracted a crowd when he went outside his home in New York. In one famous incident, a particularly eager student rushed to help the Rav get into his car and in doing so, slammed the door shut on Rav Moshe's finger. The Rav did not cry out – indeed, he did not react at all and the other occupants of the car did not realize what had happened until the car had driven several blocks and Rav Moshe opened the door to relieve his finger. While a doctor treated the wound, an astonished student asked how it could be that Rav Moshe uttered no expression of pain when the door was closed on his hand. Rav Moshe was reportedly taken aback by the question: "What? And embarrass that young man in public? *Chas veshalom!* (Heaven forbid!)" Most of us would have struggled not to swear or shout epithets at the offending student. Rav Moshe's level of self-control was considerably more refined.

YOU'RE SO BAD? YOU CAN BECOME GOOD AGAIN.

Faced with so many daily body-soul struggles, we inevitably make the wrong choice once in awhile. Sometimes my mistakes hurt me alone, but at other times they hurt others. In all cases, my decision to listen to my body instead of my soul – in other words, to choose wrongly – leaves me in a state of "wrongness." I am now a "wrong" or "bad" person, according to the magnitude of the deed.

The way to correct the situation and make myself right and "good" again is to restore the situation to its pre-mistake balance. For instance, if my mistake was to eat a meal like an animal and not like a connoisseur, I can correct the situation by internalizing the meaning of what I have done and committing myself to make the right choice in the future. Of course, the only way I can know for sure that I have fully corrected the mistake is when I find myself in exactly the same situation again with the same bodily, material temptation and choose to listen to my soul this time around.

If I make a mistake in my treatment of another person, I must also make full amends to the person. For instance, if I stole something from him, I must return the item or its value. But paying him back materially only restores the material balance to the relationship. Chances are my bad choice caused emotional damage as well. The emotional balance is restored only when the person forgives me.

From this framework, Judaism draws powerful practical suggestions.

First, because of our near enslavement to our bodies, we find it excruciatingly difficult to say two particular two-word phrases: "I'm wrong" and "I'm sorry." The reason we find these two phrases so difficult is that we live in a society that does not acknowledge the body-soul duality. Society says, "You are a body and therefore it is very important that your body be beautiful – you must look good. Alternatively, a person who recognizes that the body houses a soul, which is the true self, will focus on making the soul beautiful, even at the expense of the body's appearance to others – you must be good.

Therefore, in order to be a good person, one absolutely must master the art of saying "I'm wrong" and "I'm sorry." Unless one is flawless, it is impossible to sustain a relationship with anyone without making occasional wrong choices which hurt the other person. The pain causes strain, but many distressed relationships can be turned around by both parties simply learning how to say these two phrases with conviction.

A person who does not know what genuine goodness is will likely expend a lot of effort trying to win the admiration of others in order to make himself feel important. We call this counterfeit pleasure "being a success." Too often in our society, you can be a good wife or husband, a good friend, a loyal human being, but if you are not "successful" you are a failure. Even though on some level everybody knows that people can appear very successful and still be the dregs of society, most people believe that if you do not appear successful, you have not made it in life.

Do not fall for "looking" good. Self-respect is the genuine pleasure. It is a basic energy we all need. Without self-respect something central about our humanity is missing. Everyone needs to feel his life has some lasting value. Even though a person may enjoy awesome material pleasure – vacations, a dream home, designer clothing – and even enviable emotional pleasure – a wonderful soul mate, great friends and children – these pleasures do not themselves prevent that moment of crisis when we say "So what! What has it all led up to? What have I done of lasting value?" To really live, we need to tap into the pleasure of being good.

One of the best ways to cultivate goodness is to reflect on the ethical choices you have made. Do this at the end of each day or week once the pain of carrying out responsibilities is gone. The next step is to look back and appreciate the meaning of living a good life and to take pleasure in the specific goodness that one has accomplished over a longer time frame.

EXERCISES

Become a connoisseur of being good:

1. Make a list of twenty things you did during the past ten years that give you a sense of accomplishment. Check those that are real pleasures (being good) and place an x next to counterfeit pleasures (looking good).

2. Find a time once a week to reflect upon the week's meaningful accomplishments. Identify how each moral choice was an opportunity to become a better person.

❧ Good Isn't Good Enough: A Path to Greatness

While goodness is measured in terms of an absolute, no human being can be absolutely good. This is because the absolute yardstick we use to measure our goodness is the Infinite Source of life – but we do have infinite *potential* for growth. One might even trick one's body, which is working against spiritual growth, by saying, "Given that I am already good (a concession to my vanity), I can nonetheless desire and strive to be *great*."

In order to become a better person requires a systematic discipline of introspection. We have a form of introspection-meditation used by some of the great Jewish mystics. To enable deep introspection, they would isolate themselves from others. The Ba'al Shem Tov used to seek solitude in the Russian forest. Modern psychology has tapped into this principle with the isolation tank. An isolation tank is a pool of water that is exactly body temperature and exactly body density, which means you float in it effortlessly like in the Dead Sea, and you feel no sensation in your skin because it's your own temperature. The room is absolutely dark and there is no sound. So what do you have left after you've taken away physical sensation and sound and light? You are left with your thoughts.

We call introspection-meditation *hisbodedus*, which literally means "isolation." Practically speaking, introspection is indeed most effective in isolation – away from interruptions and distractions. Of course, isolation tanks and forests are not required. One can introspect in any suitable place of isolation. Nor does one need to devote long periods of time to hisbodedus. While some Chassidic masters recommend up to an hour a day, the average person will benefit from even a few daily minutes.

It is crucial, however, that those five or so minutes be uninterrupted. It is also very helpful that one's daily hisbodedus be at the same time and location. Spend those five minutes asking and answering one or more deeply personal questions. Rabbi Aryeh Kaplan suggests the following as examples:

- *What do I want out of life?*
- *What gives my life meaning?*
- *What is the purpose/meaning of life in general?*
- *If I could redo my life until now, what would I change?*
- *What would I be willing to die for?*
- *What would bring me more happiness than anything else in the world?*[2]

At the end of this introspection, turn your heart to Hashem and beg for help in living up to your potential. (This plea could and should be repeated at the end of the *Amida*.) The greatest benefits of this hisbodedus come with daily practice. One should therefore strive to set aside a daily time for it.

EXERCISE

Try hisbodedus for five minutes a day, at the same time and place. It is not necessary to ask and answer all of the questions listed above, although you may find it useful to do so. At the end of each session (or even during), jot down a few notes about your answers.

Prior to your five-minute hisbodedus session, remind yourself: by introspecting and working on the "big questions", you are actualizing your spiritual potential. This prep brings you one step closer to fulfillment of your life's purpose.

THE MEDIUM IS THE MESSAGE

The exercise of hisbodedus can lead to a deeper self-awareness. Still, as demonstrated at the beginning of this chapter, clear information about oneself is not very useful without an objective standard of goodness. We further defined the ultimate standard as the Infinite, unchanging Source Himself.

---

2. Aryeh Kaplan, *Jewish Meditation*, p. 17.

This standard of morality leaves a major hurdle to overcome. The philosophical framework of Chapter Two posited that this something we are calling Infinite that created this universe is unknowable by finite beings such as we. How, then, can it serve as a useful standard of goodness?

Recall the reason that Judaism uses to explain, as it were, the creation of this finite universe, the ultimate act of altruism, executed completely for the self-fulfillment of the creatures in that universe. According to this philosophy, one might well wonder what kind of altruist gives someone a complicated and potentially dangerous machine without instructions.

> This life is a test: this is only a test. Do not attempt
> to adjust your life. If this had been a real life, you
> would have been provided with instructions...
>   – anonymous

However, we do have such an instruction book. It is called "Torah." The word literally means "guide" or "instructions." Some people think it means "Bible" or "law" but these are mistranslations. The full name is *Toras Chayim* – Guidebook to Life.[3] It is, someone once remarked, the original *Life's Little Instruction Book*.[4]

Practically speaking, centuries of exile and persecution have dealt a heavy blow to Torah knowledge and we no longer know how to access its wisdom on every detail of life. Today, if you want to know how to make money, go to business school, and if you want to learn how to heal people, go to medical school. But if you want to know how to enjoy your money, how to pursue happiness, it is possible to find tremendous guidance in the Torah. As a guidebook, the Torah is relevant and belongs to every Jew,

---

3.   Cf. *Gur Aryeh* on *Bereishis* 1:1.
4.   A 1991 bestseller, with over five million copies sold.

regardless of whether or not he calls himself "religious."[5] Like any guidebook, it can be used by each person differently but is obviously useless to one who does not examine it.

Since Torah includes *Torah shebe'al peh* (the Oral Torah), in order to live a fully ethical life, one must of course learn the entire Oral Torah. This requirement poses a challenge for most of us, either because we don't have the smarts or because we lack the time.

Therefore, the only solution for most of us is to seek the help of a scholar to learn what the Torah says about our particular ethical situations. The average *ba'alabos* (householder) who is not asking a rabbi regular *she'eilos* (halachic questions) perhaps once a month (minimum) is risking committing numerous *aveiros, chas veshalom*, in all areas of life, not just about Shabbos and kashrus but about family, work and other everyday choices.

For instance, let's say we accept that it is important to *daven* in a *minyan* (quorum). But what if my wife is exhausted – should I daven at home and keep an eye on the kids, or just wish her good luck? How many men have asked this question of a rav? A woman does amazing *chessed* (acts of kindness) all over town but is too tired in the evening for her husband – how many women have asked?

❧ Transcendental Goodness

With or without the Torah, one continues to face moral choices every day. When confronting these daily dilemmas produced by the soul-body struggle, pause for a moment and recall that the Infinite Source of existence must also be the source of this dilemma. In other words, the sister tempted to hit her brother should think: "I was given this moral choice in order to make me a better person! *Wow!* What a wonderful gift!"

---

5. When teaching beginners, it is important to explain that "Torah" refers to both the *Tanach* (Written Torah) and the *Torah shebe'al peh*, which includes the Talmud, *Midrash* and Kabbala.

Thus, each moral choice, from the most minute to the most grave, can become a moment of deveikus as well. Every time I confront my own shortcomings and attempt to mend them, I can recall that this situation itself is a gift from Hashem in order to make me a better person: a personalized, transcendental gift. That idea is truly amazing to consider.

Chapter 8

Creativity

The Art of Tefilla

- *Effort and Reward of Creativity*
- *Transcendental Creativity*
- *Life Meditation (the Amida)*
- *Karma*
- *Structure of the Amida*
- *Yin-Yang Theory*
- *Sea Change*
- *Ultimate Creativity*
- *Solitary versus Group Power*

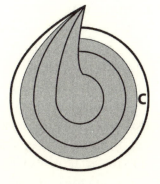

A favorite saying of Rava: "The goal of wisdom is *teshuva*..."
– Berachos 17a

Perhaps the supreme act of creativity would be the creation of a world – a Bereishis, something from absolutely nothing. As far as we know, only an Infinite Creator can do that. Human beings are creative when we make something productive and useful from that which is inert. For example, we transform iron and other elements into a 747 that can transport people from one place to another. Or we spread a palette of formless paint onto canvas to create a beautiful scene.

The ultimate creativity available to us is the creation and transformation of people. This creativity is qualitatively superior to self-transformation. After all, what rank would most people rather hold in the army, that of private or general? Even though the army could not function without soldiers who play a vital and meaningful role in defending the country, there is a greater degree of satisfaction in being a general, because that position allows greater creativity than simply following orders. The same rules apply to a business: higher levels of responsibility can be more pleasurable in their own right, regardless of the greater compensation.

➦ Effort and Reward of Creativity

Recall the struggle required to achieve personal morality: overcoming the trap of public image, to do what is good rather than what looks good. Similarly, the effort and real joy of social creativity is to conduct the orchestra for the music and not for the power trip. Any position of power can induce one to focus on controlling others rather than helping them.

Control is, of course, a factor in creativity – one must control the creative act to some degree (for instance, the artist must exert control over eye, arm, and brush in order to translate ideas into material reality). But people sometimes make the mistake of confusing the material pleasure of control with the spiritual pleasure of creativity. Stalin, Pol Pot, Saddam and a long list of other tyrants went for control – i.e., power – but their pleasure was only material, illusory creativity. Spiritual (real) creativity requires that the focus be on helping others raise themselves.

The way to tell if you are being creative or simply controlling is by analyzing your intentions: how would you feel if someone else took over and completed the job? You can also look at the results: whereas spiritual creativity gives other people pleasure, control makes only you feel powerful.[1] Jewish tradition maintains that helping someone for whom we care is the greatest earthly pleasure we can have.[2] If so, cultivating love and compassion for others must be a prerequisite to this creative pleasure.

EXERCISES

1. List five situations in which you are or were in a position of power over others, or in which someone else is or was in a position of power over you. Check those that were creative experiences and those that were controlling power trips.
2. What are the characteristics of an ideal leader?

☙ Transcendental Creativity

The transcendental dimension of creativity has two facets: appreciation and imitation. Appreciation on this level is no different from previous areas discussed. While helping others, the ultimate pleasure comes from being thankful for the ability and wherewithal to do so. The creative pleasure instantly becomes a transcendental experience too.

Now, since Hashem is the ultimate Creator, to be creative is to be most God-like. A person who strives to help others is imitating God. Ergo, the greatest creative pleasure is found in the greatest altruism, and in this regard a person imitates the Infinite – the ultimate altruistic Giver.

The hurdle that prevents many people from reaching their fullest creative potential is the steady corruption of the psyche by years of bodily, material experiences, which cloud one's ability to tap into one's true inner nature. There are temporary meditative solutions that allow momentary clarity. However, to completely

---

1. For a cogent contrast between Jewish and modernist philosophies of creativity, see Rabbi Joseph B. Soloveitchik., *Halachic Man*, pp. 99–137.
2. *Nefesh HaChayim* 2:11 (near end).

reprogram the psyche according to the ideal Infinite model requires a daily "surgical" meditation that can slice through the layers of ego and unveil the shining creative self within.

➤ Life Meditation (the Amida)

The Life Meditation comes as a response to this need for a systematic way to reach our individual and collective potential. Prior to and during the First Temple era, when classical Hebrew was still spoken and prophecy was as common as grape vines, there were many keys available to unlock the inner creative self. After the destruction and exile circa 350 B.C.E., the *Anshei Knesses HaGedola* faced three problems: Jews were now scattered around the world, having lost touch with each other; Hebrew was no longer a mother tongue; and the Jewish meditative arts were being forgotten. In addition to the berachos, the Sages created the mantra-like "life" meditation, the Amida (lit.: standing). In contrast to ordinary, brief mantras that are personalized, the Amida is an intricate "mantra" for all Jews to say every day. It is written in classical Hebrew and is thereby able to encapsulate some of the most esoteric concepts. Three of the sages of the Knesses HaGedola were certified prophets, which means that this life meditation is also, to some extent, written in the language of prophecy.[3]

EXTERNAL STRUCTURE

Recall the concept of the beracha as the archetypal transcendental moment. A single beracha elevates one narrowly defined experience to the transcendental realm of deveikus.

The Amida is a series of eighteen berachos (technically we added one to make nineteen, but the fact that we still call the Amida "*Shemoneh Esrei*" indicates that the *essence* of the Amida is eighteen). In gematria, eighteen (*ches*-8 + *yud*-10) represents *chai* (life). Each beracha in the meditation operates within a specific area of consciousness and transcendence. Under deep analysis,

---

3. Haggai, Zecharia and Nehemia (mentioned frequently in the Talmud).

their pattern also mirrors human history as well as an individual's life cycle. On the simplest level, this string of eighteen berachos is a tremendous key to unlocking human potential.[4]

In some ways, the Amida is the counterpart of the Shema. Their contrasting qualities complement each other:

	SHEMA UNITY MEDITATION	AMIDA LIFE MEDITATION
Method	transcend this world	fully focus on this world
Metaphor	go "up" to God	bring God "down"
Result	nullify self	transform self
Psychology	Receive and give love	self-analysis

Whereas the Shema opens the gates of pure love for us, the Amida is more like a full psychoanalysis. In Hebrew this meditation is sometimes called *his-pa-leil*, which literally means, "examine oneself." This term reflects the concept that nothing we say will change God. By definition, Hashem is unchanging. This unusual "mantra" is a complex meditation that, compared to the Shema, takes tremendous time and self-discipline for success.

THE AMIDA AS A "MANTRA"

How does the Amida compare to an ordinary mantra? An ordinary mantra is a short phrase repeated over and over to train the mind toward certain thought patterns and away from others.

4. *Shabbos* 10a describes tefilla as *"chayei sha'ah."*

Typically, a person will sit for 30–60 minutes saying a mantra hundreds of times until the words become the mind's sole focus. Having thus internalized the words, one continues to repeat them throughout the day in a continuous effort to control the mind.

The Jewish version of this type of mantra meditation is called *higayon* (see chart in Appendix D). The Amida is somewhat different. Contrast:

	SIMPLE MANTRA (higayon)	AMIDA (hispaleil)
length	Short phrase (2–10 words) conveying one main idea	Long series of phrases (650–700 words), which convey many complex nuances of one main idea
times per session	Hundreds	1
times per day	Thousands	1–4

The Amida is customarily repeated several times a day. In that sense it resembles a mantra. Those who make the effort to use it daily usually come to memorize it. They can then begin to see the meditation as an organic whole, repeated over and over throughout one's life, each time taking one to deeper and deeper levels of self-consciousness and higher and higher planes of transcendence.

It would be unrealistic to repeat this meditation much more often. It is too difficult. To say it once can take anywhere from five to twenty minutes, depending on one's personal rhythm.[5]

---

5. However, there is no formal limit; this estimate is based on nonscientific observation.

Moreover, to say it with proper kavana requires a warm-up and warm-down.

As a "mantra," the Amida is a key to unlock the door to the inner self. Unlike the Eastern mantra, it does not serve primarily for mental discipline. The discipline of saying it daily results in an emotional, cathartic cleansing. Western culture offers catharsis mainly via theater and spectator sport; the Jewish seeker finds it within the self and in a daily struggle to become a greater human being.

Whereas the goal of the Eastern mantra is to learn *how to be* and Typical prayer is for *hoping for something I lack*, the Amida – indeed, all of Jewish spirituality ultimately – is about *becoming*.[6]

This distinction explains the enigmatic form of the Amida. Rather than repeat a short phrase hundreds of times, we say a very long phrase only once. While repetitive and vocalized like a simple mantra (*higayon*), the Amida is much longer and expresses complex ideas. Semantically, these ideas resemble supplicatory prayer, which is the stereotypical Western meditation. In other words, the Amida looks like a mantra that is expressed like a prayer or like a prayer that is said repetitively like a mantra.

THE AMIDA AS A PRAYER

Western prayer has two defining elements:

1. petitioning to receive something
2. pouring out one's emotions

To whom are we petitioning? To Hashem? Asking the Infinite Creator to give differently or to give something that does not exist is philosophically difficult. Are we asking the unchanging Infinite to change to match our desires?

How, then, can we pray? Can we ask Hashem for anything?

6. Rabbi Nathan T. Cardozo, *Critique of Western Civilization*.

To ask for something implies that I want the giver to change his current intentions. If he already plans to give me something, why bother to ask? And if he does not plan to give it to me, how will it help to ask? Again, Hashem by definition is unchanging.

It would seem that, according to the Jewish concept of transcendence, our conventional notion of "prayer" makes no sense. Instead, when we examine ourselves (*hispaleil*) in *the* Amida-meditation, we are attempting to change ourselves in order to mirror Hashem better.[7]

As for the second element of prayer, pouring out one's emotions, the Amida can do just that. Saying the Amida well, with the right kavanos, can significantly increase deveikus. This closeness results from a combination of focused attention and increased calmness.[8]

An analogy: Imagine walking through a dark tunnel with a trail of small buttons on the ground. Each button, when stepped on, generates a small amount of electricity, which is then stored in a battery. Yet the buttons are so small that it takes concentration to step on each one. You can walk through the tunnel without stepping on any, or you may step on a few or even all. At the end of the tunnel, there is a light bulb. The last button is the switch to release the electricity stored in the battery and illuminate the way. Depending on how well you walked the tunnel, you may have anywhere from no light to much light.

The parable describes how this Jewish "mantra" works. At the end of the Amida, the meditator is "plugged in" to Hashem to the degree that s/he navigated the meditation with kavana. At that final moment, when the light bulb goes on, so to speak, the meditator has a golden moment to use that light to look within him/herself.[9]

---

7. More precisely, the purpose of the lacking is specifically to produce this relationship of asking and giving (*Nefesh HaChayim* 2:4).
8. *Eitz Chayim* 61.
9. *Ibid.*

Please recall from previous chapters the term for plugging-in: deveikus. This controlled deveikus experience teaches us experientially the transcendental meaning of being alive. When practiced regularly, one learns over time to connect just as deeply in other, more mundane settings, adding "real life" (i.e., transcendental awareness) to one's life.[10] Just as the body is sustained by continuous breathing, the soul thrives via life meditation.[11]

The actual technique is described below.

➤ Karma

There is a mainstream opinion in Jewish tradition that each soul enters this world with a mission, often to work out certain unresolved problems from a past life.[12] The Sanskrit word karma, referring to these challenges, has entered the English language. One's karma also includes new difficulties that arise during this lifetime.[13]

Every challenge that we encounter in life is due to karma.[14] As we grow and work out the karma, certain challenges disappear. So, for instance, a theoretical person with no negative karma – a totally righteous person – would always get whatever s/he needs whenever s/he needs it. As one of my teachers explained, "When a tzaddik reaches into his pocket he always pulls out the correct change."[15] Therefore, all of life's ups and downs start to make sense. Challenges are opportunities to work out my karma. If I

---

10. *Shabbos* 10a describes tefilla as "*chayei sha'ah*."
11. Rabbi Shimshon Pincus, *Sha'arim BeTefilla*, p. 17.
12. See Arizal, *Sha'ar HaGilgul*.
13. *Nefesh HaChayim*, ch. 1. See discussion of pain in Chapter 5. "Karma" is the correct English word (borrowed from Sanskrit) for this principle of *mida-k'neged-mida* (cause and effect) in both the physical and metaphysical planes of existence.
14. See Rashi's comment to *Koheles* 3:11.
15. A new soul may not have karmic issues, and would have to seek other reasons for its birth. However, according to the Arizal (*Sha'ar HaGilgul*), there have been very few new souls born since the destruction of the Second Temple (70 C.E.).

succeed in letting go of whatever I was clinging to and generating that karma, the challenge goes away. In other words, I do not change the unchanging Infinite Creator; I change myself and this new reality of my self "allows" Hashem to treat me according to a different set of rules.

For example, imagine a person who lost her job and can't find another. Perhaps her karma that she needs to work out at that moment is her emotional attachment to employment. When she meditates, attaching her mind and heart to God, pours out her heart and finally detaches herself from "needing" a job, she has now changed her karma. There is no longer any karmic need for her to be without work and she will now find work. It's a simplified example, but essentially true; the hard part is to take that real step of growth, and it may take her days or weeks of meditation to succeed. But over time, with much practice, one should be able to succeed after just a few meditation sessions – and most people do.

In a nutshell, the Amida is a Jewish approach to "how to get your prayers answered."[16] Now, most people are aware of a distinction between the person they are now and the person they have the potential to be. We constantly strive for this ideal and usually fall short. Why do we fail? Usually because we lack clarity about the ideal itself. Most of us lack the wisdom to visualize a true ideal.

This "master mantra" is a road map to the ideal spiritual person.

➥ Structure of the Amida

The Amida meditation is a string of eighteen berachos. These eighteen form three distinct groups: the first three, the middle twelve and the last three. Approximately 1,800 years ago (500 years after the Amida was composed), the sages of the time added a thir-

---

16. Ralbag, quoted in Pliskin, *Consulting the Wise*, p. 75. See *Nefesh HaChayim* 3:2:4.

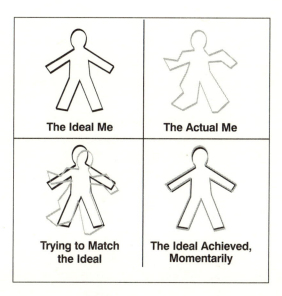

| The Ideal Me | The Actual Me |
| Trying to Match the Ideal | The Ideal Achieved, Momentarily |

teenth beracha to the middle group. The number 13 alludes to unity and love (see Chapter Six).

The first group establishes our bearings within the transcendental field, the middle group develops the transcendence until a climax at the fifteenth beracha, and the final group of three berachos forms the conclusion.

Unlike the berachos discussed in Chapter Five, each of these nineteen is an entire paragraph. Each paragraph ends with the familiar language, "BORUCH ATOH ADONOI..." To understand the purpose and ideal kavana of each beracha, one must study the entire paragraph – a larger task than the scope of this book. The Talmud allows for beginners to say it in any language they understand; therefore, anyone who finds the full Hebrew text overwhelming should feel completely at ease to begin a daily Amida practice with an English version.[17] The text is given at the end of this chapter.

At this point, it is instructive to look at the last beracha of

17. *Berachos* 40b; *Shavuos* 39a; *Sotah* 33a; Cf. *Magen Avraham* on *Shulchan Aruch Orach Chaim* 62:1.

the middle group, which is in some ways the climax of the entire mantra. The fifteen previous berachos all build toward it, and the final three berachos are all concluding echoes after it. The tag-line of this climactic beracha reads:

BORUCH ATOH ADONOI SHO-MEI-AH TEFILLA.

You the Infinite are the Source, open to human transcendence.

In other words, at the highest moment of transcendence during one of Judaism's central meditations, the kavana is to internalize the amazing possibility and the actuality of transcendence itself. Complete knowledge of this fact – the fact that we can transcend, that we can connect to God – is synonymous with transcendence itself and is therefore the object of our meditation.

The full Amida can be an amazing, transformative experience. However, it is almost overwhelmingly long and complex. Begin, then, with the first beracha alone. Indeed, the first beracha contains the lion's share of the cosmic depth and power found in the entire meditation. It may be a worthwhile long-term goal to learn the full meditation. But in the meantime, the first beracha will give you a lot of mileage.

THE FIRST BERACHA

The first beracha is akin to turning on the power. Its tag reads:

BORUCH ATOH ADONOI MOH-GEIN AVROHOM.

You, the Infinite, are the source, the shield (protection and badge) of Avraham.

What does Avraham have to do with our meditation? If we say this with concentration, we kindle emotions based on what we know about the life and personality of Avraham. We actually know much about the life of Avraham. Among other things, we know that he is considered the father of the three monotheistic religions, which account for a third of humanity, and he may be a progenitor of eastern spirituality as well.[18] Whatever fueled him may be something worth plugging into.

But we also know that Avraham's wife, Sarah, was equally important as a spiritual innovator. In fact, she was in some ways his spiritual superior.[19] Yet, the Amida mentions Avraham but not Sarah. This subtle issue needs some explanation.

➥ Yin-Yang Theory

It is a basic principle of classical Judaism that not only is there no inequality between men and women, but also on an idealized spiritual plane there is no difference between them. Ideally, a man and woman are a single soul (*neshama*) that was separated at some time past into two and whose mission it is to find each other and become one again. We learn this concept from the story of the Garden of Eden, when the first human, Adam, is split in two. In fact, according to Jewish tradition, before the split, Adam is a person with both male and female characteristics. After the split, Adam and Chava are differentiated by gender.[20]

Therefore, when a man and a woman have an ideal marriage, they again become one soul. This concept is not simply poetic. Their souls actually merge. Yet, the fact that man and woman were once a single soul and can become a single soul again does not mean that they are identical. Nor do they have the same roles in life. Similarly, although Sarah the individual was a greater mystic than Avraham, it does not mean that their spiritual natures were similar. Rather, men and women usually possess spiritually distinct natures that are generally stereotyped, to borrow from Eastern vocabulary, as the *yin* (feminine) and the *yang* (masculine). Each person, whether female or male, possesses some mixture of the two tendencies. According to Chinese yin-yang theory, the

18. See A. Seinfeld, *The Art of Amazement*, ch. 1.
19. *Bereishis* 21:12. See FN 39 below.
20. *Berachos* 61a.

feminine yin is characterized by internality, darkness, peace, and the Earth; the male yang is characterized by externality, light, agitation, and the Heavens.

Many ancient cultures developed variations on this theme and many modern religious groups have appropriated these symbols for their own purposes. Traditionally, however, the familiar yin-yang symbol of blackness and whiteness in flux represents the basic theory of a yin-yang ideal of these two forces in balance. Some readers at this point reach a cognitive impasse. The idea that there are significant differences between men and women has been nearly drummed out of our consciousness. In stark contrast, however, Judaism maintains that the obvious physical differences between men and women do represent similar hormonal, psychological and mental differences as well. This traditional view has been somewhat rehabilitated in recent years thanks to the success of John Gray's book, *Men Are From Mars, Women Are From Venus*, a work which is generally consistent with Jewish tradition.[21]

The Jewish model of the male-female dynamic begins with the simple yin-yang concept of complementary energies. However, the full picture is more complex. The interaction of the two is the diametric opposite of their natures. Thus, woman and man might be compared to a cup and water. The cup holds the water. The interaction of the cup to the water is described as the cup holding or containing the water. Therefore, in terms of their interaction, the cup is the external and the water the internal.

However, the cup itself is "internal-looking." The cup's essence is defined by what is inside. We may decorate the cup, but

---

21. "Unlike its mathematical counterpart, ontological equality is not expressed in sameness or identity. While the Torah, assuredly, does not discriminate against men or women, undoubtedly it does discriminate between them" (Rabbi Mayer Twersky, attributed). See also the great Torah-based books on this theme: Rabbi Yirmiyahu and Tehilla Abramov, *Two Halves of a Whole: Torah Guidelines for Marriage* (Southfield, Mich.: Targum, 1994) and Gila Manolson, *Outside/Inside: A Fresh Look at Tsniut* (Southfield, Mich.: Targum, 2005).

its real value qua cup is in what it can do on the inside, not how it appears on the outside. The water is the exact opposite. When interacting with the cup, the water is surrounded and protected by the cup. But by itself, the water is only relevant in its externality. If we look at the internal nature of water, we see two abundant elements, hydrogen and oxygen. We don't value water for these elements. We value it as water; we want to know if it's frozen, liquid or gas, hot or cold, pure or dirty, all externally observable features.

The cup and water resemble the feminine and masculine principles.

First, consider the interaction of the feminine and the masculine. In the relationship between woman and man, the external, enveloping feminine interacts with the internal, enveloped masculine. We observe this interaction on the biological level and it is mirrored in Jewish custom: the bride at a traditional wedding walks around the groom and not vice-versa. The man is like water: boundless, groundless and shapeless until the woman gives him bounds, grounding and shape; in lay terms, he is homeless until she gives him a home.

BALANCE OF ENERGY   INTERACTION

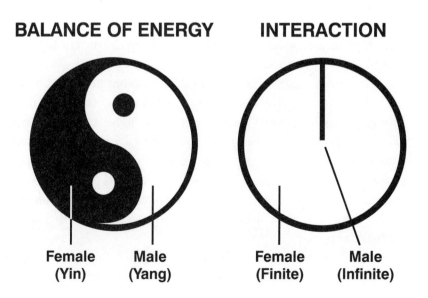

| Female | Male | Female | Male |
| (Yin) | (Yang) | (Finite) | (Infinite) |

Similarly, when we describe how Hashem interacts with the finite universe we use the symbolism of male energy entering female energy, so to speak. Hashem actively "dwells," as it were, in the world. However, like the cup and water, feminine and masculine natures in themselves are the opposite of their interactions: the female can only surround the male because of her essential internality. Conversely, the male seeks refuge in her internality because he is an essentially external being.

One finds greater spiritual strength by harnessing one's essence; therefore, feminine spiritual strength comes largely from that which she keeps hidden and masculine strength from that which he reveals.

Let us apply this model to the story of Adam and Chava. Adam begins with both male and female characteristics (*Bereishis* 1:27). Gender appears when this hermaphroditic creature called Adam is split into two, male and female (*Bereishis* 2:21–22). Which of the two halves should we expect to retain the original name, Adam?

A name is an external representation of something. The half of this yin-yang duality that retains the external expression of their total spiritual essence is by definition male. Therefore, the original name for the total being, *Adam*, remains with the male half. The female aspect becomes his *ezer kenegdo*, or "contrasting complement" (*Bereishis* 2:20).

This story needs careful elaboration to avoid misunderstanding. To call woman the "contrasting complement" (or "helpmate" in some translations) of man is not a statement of contrasting value. On the contrary, her role is as essential as his in their self-actualization. Without her, he'll never amount to anything. Man's problem is that alone, he is essentially unfulfilled potential. Man qua man is a creative idea, a blueprint; woman takes his potential, his idea, his blueprint, and builds it into something real. That is her special power.

This differentiation is fully expressed in human reproduction, where the only thing that a man has to offer is a seed, a tiny drop so small that it's almost nothing, almost the smallest unit of information that he can produce. He gives that seed to a woman who then builds it into something he could never build – another human being. Without her, his ultimate creative potential is worthless. Together, when they become one, their creative potential is nearly boundless.

This model explains the roles portrayed in *Bereishis* 18, where Avraham runs outside the tent and Sarah remains inside. Both are equally important in the story, but each represents an energy that complements the other. They are two sides of a coin, one visible and one hidden. We know that Sarah is part of the equation and it is no slight to her honor to be the keeper of the internal wisdom. But her mystical strength depends on her role as the hidden, internal side of the yin-yang, just as Avraham's strength depends on his role in the external world. Both halves are essential for a complete being.

Now it is possible to understand the focus in this meditation on Avraham, and, to a lesser extent, on Yitzchak and Yaakov.

The Amida takes one into the very essence of transcendence. That essence is expressed with a chain of ideas, as discussed above. The three forefathers – Avraham, Yitzchak and Yaakov – gave the Jewish people and the world specific potentialities that constitute our greatness as a people and as a species:

- Avraham – lovingkindness
- Yitzchak – pure transcendence
- Yaakov – perfect harmony of heaven and earth.

Yet where are the complementary wives – Sarah, Rivka, Rachel and Leah? Did they not also contribute to our spiritual potential?

The answer should now be clear. We do not mention the foremothers by name because, while each made a unique contribution, their spiritual essences are intertwined with their husbands'. To name them in a transcendent, unifying meditation would be redundant.

Tragically, this spiritual differentiation has often been mis-used to take advantage of women economically and politically. It is no less unfortunate that generations have been educated to be-lieve that women and men are essentially the same, when in fact we are complementary.

Sarah's dominant character trait is *din*, strict justice. Her pri-mary spiritual mission is to shape Avraham's kindness. She is the one who initiated the banishment of Avraham's wayward son Ish-mael; Avraham would never have done so on his own. The Torah is unequivocal on this: "Whatever Sarah will say to you, heed her voice."[22] Sarah is right. Avraham needs to absorb that measure of *din* from her.

A similar pattern occurs with Yitzchak and Rivka. Here, the tables are turned: Yitzchak, the quintessential transcendental man, is too severe with Yaakov *(Bereishis* 25:28). It takes Rivka's special sensitivity and kindness to rescue Yaakov *(Bereishis* 27), instructing him to trick Yitzchak into giving him his due blessing. In hindsight, Yaakov accepts this turn of events as correct *(Bereishis* 28), when he ratifies the earlier blessing. Like Sarah, we see Rivka's historical role completely enmeshed with and complementary to her husband's.

As for Yaakov and his two wives, Rachel and Leah, the pat-tern shifts slightly. For Yaakov has no fundamental lack: the Torah calls him *ish tam*, "a perfect man."[23] Rather than complement him, his wives protect him from the outside world. They help Yaakov disentangle the family from their malevolent father, Laban, saying, "We have nothing more to do with him and we are with you." This statement of support demarcates a clear emotional and physical boundary around Yaakov (and the Jewish people, whom Yaakov represents).[24]

This model is the source of the Jewish custom mentioned above that a bride encircles her groom under the wedding canopy,

22. *Bereishis* 12:12.
23. *Ibid.* 25:27.
24. *Ibid.* 31:14–16.

symbolizing her spiritual protection of him. Because the pattern set by Yaakov, Rachel, and Leah is our ideal model, Jews have always been called "children of Yaakov" or "children of Israel" (Yaakov's second name – see Chapter Two).

In accordance with the radio analogy, when we say the first beracha, we've switched on the power. Avraham (with Sarah) represents the transcendental connection in the most general way. Avraham's legacy is our collective ability to stretch ourselves toward Infinity, via most of the world's meditative traditions. Transcendence as we know it is an Avrahamic concept. It is Avraham's badge, as it were, or, in classical terms, his shield; hence, the first beracha of the Amida meditation: "...*moh-gein Avrohom* – shield of Avraham."

LIFE MEDITATION – THE FIRST BERACHA

Boruch atoh Adonoi Eloheinu ve-Elohei avoseinu:
You, the Infinite, are the Source, our power and the power of our ancestors:

Elohei Av-roh-hohm,
The power of Avraham (lovingkindness balanced with justice),

Elohei Yitz-chohk,
the power of Yitzchak (strict truth, balanced with compassion),

ve-Elohei Ya-akov;
and the power of Yaakov (human excellence, harmony of heaven and earth);

ho-Eil ha-goh-dol ha-gee-bor, v'ha-no-roh Eil el-yon,
the power that is great (big), mighty (valiant) and awesome (breathtaking), the highest power,

---

go-meil cha-soh-deem to-veem v-ko-nei ha-kol;
> *the Insurer of many acts of kindness and the invisible Hand behind everything;*

ve-zo-cheir chas-dei oh-vos
> *the fulfiller of the good karma of the forebears*

u-mei-vee go-eil lee-v'nei v'nei-hem
> *and bringer of enlightenment to their children's children*

l'ma-an sh-mo, b'a-ha-voh.
> *for the sake of its essence, with love.*

Melech,
> *Director (the invisible Hand, to the extent that we allow it),*

ozeir,
> *helper (wherever we need help),*

u-mo-shee-a
> *resuscitator (giving us clarity of reality),*

u-moh-gein...
> *and shield (both in the sense of protection and as a spiritual badge)*

Boh-ruch atoh Ado-noi moh-gein Av-roh-hohm.
> *You the Infinite are the source, the shield (protection and badge) of Avraham.*

❧ Sea Change

When used well, the Amida causes a growth spurt every time. In fact, there is a Chassidic tradition that someone who completes the Amida and is the same person afterward hasn't said it with kavana.[25] The way to effect such a sea change, whether one says the full mantra or only the first beracha, is to use the clarity it provides to access one's feelings. At the end of the recitation – before leaving the meditative posture – let the heart start talking. Express whatever it is that you have been feeling this morning, today, this week, this month. The expression may be, "I'm so lonely, help me overcome this loneliness"; or "I need to pass the exam, help me pass"; or "I'm getting angry so easily, help me learn to be patient." The expression often takes the form of a supplication because that form is particularly useful for bringing up the deepest emotions.

We do not need to think, however, that we are asking for favors. Remember, Hashem is everywhere all the time. When we achieve a degree of deveikus, we are beyond passing exams. That is not an issue. What is at stake is who we are as people, our attachment to passing the exam. The result of pouring out the little prayer at the end of the Amida should be that the sense of fear, urgency or whatever it was that produced the prayer goes away, replaced by a stronger sense of amazing awareness.[26] If the issue is a personality trait, such as patience or joy, this practice will slowly internalize the change one is seeking to make.

TECHNIQUES

The techniques for saying the Amida all enhance and accelerate its benefits.[27] The guiding principle should be to maximize our sense of awe, for awe (amazement) is what opens the doors of perception. As with the Krias Shema, one should strive to memorize

25. Attributed to the Ba'al Shem Tov.
26. Rabbi Shimshon Pincus, *Sha'arim BeTefilla*, pp. 26–55; 130; 180–83.
27. Cf. *Berachos* 31a.

the Amida. Memorization will occur almost effortlessly over the course of a few months for those who have the self-discipline to say it daily.

POSITION

The Amida can be said in any position, but it is best to stand with the feet together, knees slightly bent and body slightly leaning forward. The rabbis use the analogy of a king.[28] Imagine how you would stand in front of the most awesome king – say Shlomo HaMelech or Paroh or any monarch that you can imagine. That sense of awe is a fraction of what we should feel "standing before" the Infinite Creator. The posture helps generate this emotional attitude.

The hands should be held close to the body, but not with the fingers clasped. This position mimics a *malach*. A malach is a spiritual entity that has no free will (because it has no material body). It is the agent of manifestation of infinite Divine energy into the finite. Non-Jewish interpretations of the Torah have translated *malach* as "angel" and re-designed it with wings and a personality. We imitate the malach during this meditation as an additional tool to guide our kavana towards transcendence.

For greater kavana, the eyes should be closed, or, if open, gazing below eye-level, to maintain the awareness of standing before a king.

LOCATION AND TIME

The Amida works best for most people if said at a fixed time and place. Choose a time and place that will give you an undisturbed session every day. When you meditate at a fixed time you will find it very easy to increase your kavana and deepen the experience. The Chachamim (Sages) who designed the mantra designated three ideal time periods for it: early in the morning, early in the

---

28. *Berachos* 28b; *Orach Chayim* 98.

afternoon[29] and early in the evening.[30] The three ideal time periods to say the Amida imitate the time periods from the Temple service described in the Torah.[31]

The beginner would best start with any one of these time periods and to stick with it. In time, some decide to add another session. If possible, the exact location should have minimal distractions. For instance, many prefer to stand facing a blank wall. Unplug the phone. Let your family members know that you are meditating and ask them not to disturb you during this time. After a short time, you and everyone else will grow accustomed to this meditation session as a part of the daily routine.

WARM-UP AND WARM-DOWN

The Amida is mentally, emotionally and even physically challenging. Like vigorous physical exercise, it should include a warm-up and warm-down. You are about to take a profound journey; don't dive in cold. Take a few minutes before you begin in order to think about what you are about to do.[32]

Many like to use specific songs of Dovid HaMelech to stimulate the mind and emotions for the work they are about to perform. Each of these songs (or psalms) is a "thought unit" that explores the details of a single emotion, similar in length and intention to modern popular music (although incomparable in poetic depth). Many find Psalm 145 particularly suitable for such a warm-up, and it has been used as such since at least Talmudic times, and probably much longer.[33] The heart of the psalm is the verse:

29. It is appropriate any time from to thirty minutes after "true noon" (when the sun is straight overhead) until sunset.
30. If necessary, anytime at night.
31. Cf. *Bamidbar* 28; *Tehillim* 145; *Berachos* 6b.
32. Cf. Rabbi S. Pincus, *Sha'arim BeTefilla*, p. 20.
33. *Berachos* 4b.

POSAY-ACH ES YAH-DEH-CHOH,
UMASBEE-A LECHOL CHAI RATZON

Open your hands and fulfill the needs of all creatures.

The need for a warm-down depends on how vigorously you exercised. If you just read through the mantra without great concentration, you probably will need very little warm-down. But even a moderate amount of kavana warrants another psalm and perhaps the Aleinu meditation, which, besides the Shema, may be the best-known meditation in Judaism. [34]

VOICE

If we truly felt sufficiently amazed at the awesomeness of Hashem, we would be speechless. Such awe is a high ideal – we should be so overcome with emotion that we cannot find the words. Yet we are human. We are not so spiritual that we can successfully meditate in total silence. We need to utter words or else our minds will invariably wander. Therefore, the Sages instituted a balance between the awe of the heart and the needs of the mind: that is, to say the mantra in a whisper – so quietly that a person standing beside you cannot hear you. Although whispered, this remains an internal meditation and the words ultimately turn inward.[35]

34. See *Abudarham Hashaleim* (Vol 1) where he includes the Aleinu in the Yom Kippur Amida but not at the end of the daily services as we have today. It follows that it was adopted from the heart of the Yom Kippur usage into the daily service. The Aleinu therefore has a lofty origin.
35. Cf. Rabbi S. Pincus, *Sha'arim BeTefilla.*, p. 133.

EXERCISES

The Life Meditation (Amida)

   Find a quiet, undisturbed location. As with other meditation, it is preferable to say it in any language you understand
if the Hebrew comes with difficulty.

1. *To begin*: The Amida gives multifaceted expression to the
   one-pointed unity of the Shema. Say the Amida in the
   morning, immediately at the conclusion of your Shema
   meditation. Continue for four weeks.

2. *After this first month*, if you feel ready, add a second Amida
   session in the afternoon. (Some say that the afternoon
   meditation is the most powerful, and should even have
   precedence over the morning, if you only have time to
   say it once a day.)

      Say it slowly. The slower one says the Amida, the greater
   the potential benefit. Some suggest a pace of seven seconds
   per word, which brings the first paragraph to less than
   five minutes.

      If and when you get to the point of saying the full
   version of the Amida, you may complete the full meditation
   in five minutes (probably too fast) or in an hour (quite
   slow). The pace should be determined by one's ability to
   concentrate on the meaning of every word.

3. *At the conclusion of the second month*: Try to say the Amida
   in the evening. The Sages recommend a long-term goal of
   three regular meditation sessions every day. There is a very
   practical reason for this. We humans tend to be very this-
   worldly creatures, absorbed in our work, our relationships
   and our recreation. For many, just making ends meet takes
   most of the day. This reality of our lives is the antithesis of
   transcendence. Thus, in becoming transcendental beings,
   it helps to partition the day with meditation sessions: in
   the early morning before we get involved in the day's
   activities, in the afternoon, when we're most absorbed

in activities; and in the evening, at the end of a day's work.

In this way, meditation becomes a tool to help us maintain an enhanced perception throughout the day.

✿ Ultimate Creativity

Recall the Jewish concept of Hashem: an unchanging reality and the Source of all pleasures in life. If one could tap into Hashem Himself, one could theoretically experience infinite pleasure. The meditative practices of previous chapters (awareness, saying berachos with proper kavana and so on) are effective tools to find great pleasure in life's minutiae, both their finite and transcendental qualities. Although satisfying, however, those meditations are incomplete. For as much as we were created to live life for the moment, we also have a duty to participate fully in human society and human history.

It appears that most people do sense this pull, even if subconsciously. Many of us strive to leave the world a better place than we found it.[36]

Prior to the Amida, contemplate the fact that Hashem is intimately involved with every detail of your life and the world.

Paying attention to history and fixing the world are fundamental Jewish concepts, mentioned repeatedly in the sources. Since Jewish spirituality should be a holistic path (see Introduction), this duty to history is expressed in the Amida meditation itself.

This long and rich arrangement of Hebrew words can connect

36. Jews participate in grass-roots social, political, intellectual and religious movements in vastly disproportionate numbers, comprising anywhere from 20 to 50 percent of the participants in many political activities, new-age groups and academic revolutions. Some interpret this high Jewish participation as a more general Jewish drive to excel in any area of endeavor.

us not merely to the Infinite Creator qua Infinite, but to the infinity (small *i*) as expressed in this temporal world, a world where we do perceive time and history. The Amida is a subtly poetic expression of the drama of history. While any beracha can open a connection to the universe in its *current* state, the Amida (said with kavana) can connect us to the universe *as it is, was and will be* – i.e., the way that the totality of the universe would appear from Hashem's point of view, metaphorically speaking. That is transcendence.

William Faulkner wrote that "the past isn't dead; it isn't even past."[37] He meant that we who are alive right now are creating the past in our minds. Therefore, any talk of history should also talk of the human experience today. And that is indeed what we find in this master "mantra," the Amida: it addresses both our immediate personal situation and our orientation to a collective history. It simultaneously works at these two levels.

➨ Solitary versus Group Power

Meditation is one of the most personal and private acts that a person can do. To develop a successful discipline, every tradition in the world recommends meditating at a fixed time and place, with few distractions – which may include other people (as per Chapter Six). These goals bring us back to a stereotypical image of meditation, with a lone guru sitting high on a mountaintop, meditating in complete tranquility.

Jewish tradition regards strict isolationists unfavorably. While temporary isolation can be an important means of introspection (as per Chapter Seven), spirituality is supposed to be a part of everyday life, not apart from life. Proper meditation can teach us an idealized model for life. For instance:

- While berachos are designed to help us focus on and appreciate the "*Wow!*" of certain experiences, we strive

37. *Requiem for a Nun* (New York: Random House, 1950), p. 92.

to apply that same awareness and appreciation to every life experience – constant kavana.

- Once we begin to frame our day with a meditation on unity (the Shema), we should strive for unity, harmony and perfection in every action.
- Just as the Amida often works best in a group setting, so too we sometimes face our most complex and challenging activities better as a group effort, with the goal of helping each other make the journey (as opposed to competing with each other).[38]

On a practical level, the Chachomim who wrote the Amida actually recommended different dosages of meditation to men and to women. They taught men to meditate in a group. The strength of the group strengthens the individual. When we meditate regularly with a group, we are less likely to rush or to miss a session. The group also gives us the opportunity to compare techniques with other like-minded souls. To women, whom the Torah considers in certain ways more naturally transcendent than men,[39] the mystics proffer no such specific advice, although today some women find group meditation highly beneficial.[40]

To balance these needs – the individual versus the group – Judaism has developed a combined strategy. On the one hand, we meditate whenever possible in a group. On the other hand, each individual's meditation is said in a quiet whisper as the mind gazes inward.

38. Mark Verman summarizes the textual and historical basis for this principle in *The History and Varieties of Jewish Meditation*, ch. 2.
39. This general view is derived from the specific case of the matriarch Sarah. See *Bereishis* 21:12; the Talmudic discussions of a woman's greater *binah* and lighter *daas* in *Nida* 45b, *Pesachim* 88b, *Shabbos* 33b, *Kiddushin* 80b.
40. Recall the above discussion of the yin-yang relationship between men and women. Men and women are not identical; rather, we are complementary.

Unfortunately, it is not always easy to find a like-minded group. Very often, the individuals are sincere and dedicated, but they lack sufficient numbers to boost their individual efforts, or the groups will say the Amida in sufficient numbers but with poor kavana that can negatively affect the others. (I have attended minyanim where participants actually start chatting the moment they finish their silent Amida – even if others are still deep in tefilla! This is an unfortunate situation that sometimes turns people off davening altogether.)

The good news is that many Jewish communities already have one or more Jewish meditation groups which are really trying hard to help each other through a successful daily Amida session. Some of these groups are very small and pining for greater participation. Seek them out. You will both gain from and strengthen the collective power of the group and you will help strengthen the others.

Spirituality is a personal quest, yet Jewish spirituality has survived only via Jewish communities. Moreover, the commitment to group tefilla helps keep a community together. It is an interdependent relationship and a doorway open to practitioners of all degrees.

Chapter 9

Virtuosity

The Art of Becoming

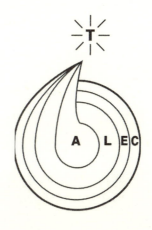

- *Pleasure versus Pain and Effort*
- *Pleasure versus Happiness*
- *Why Judaism?*
- *The Pleasure Virtuoso*

It is not in the heavens, that you
should say, "Who will go up for us
to the heavens and take it to us?
and then we will hear it and do it."
   And not across the sea, that you should say, "Who will cross
the sea for us and take it to us? and then we will hear it and do it."
But the matter is very near to you, in your mouth
and in your heart to do it (*Devarim* 30:12–14).

Pleasure versus Pain and Effort

The greatest expression of human creativity is transforming the
part of the human that resembles the animal (the body) into a

spiritual being that reflects the infinite spark within us, the soul. We have a limited time – perhaps one or two lifetimes – to accomplish this task. The basic path toward this goal is the development of an expanded consciousness, which means to master both constant awareness and transcendent kavana (deveikus).

This handbook has touched upon all the prerequisite knowledge and many of the central details necessary to develop such a consciousness. As a course of study, however, it has left two important questions unresolved:

1. Why does it need to be so hard? Most of us are just dreaming of a day at the beach. Our entire culture is geared toward retirement. The thrust of the pleasure thesis contradicts the central values of the comfort seeker.
2. Why Judaism – why should I choose this system, or any system? Maybe I will get more pleasure if I discover my own path.

In terms of effort, the art of kavana actually requires two types of effort:

1. learning *how* to enjoy the activity (becoming a connoisseur); and
2. actually doing it (controlling the body's pull toward materialism).

The bottom line is that pleasure is hard work. This factor distinguishes pleasure from comfort, which by definition is a lack of work. Consider the fact that some people go to the trouble of cultivating a taste for fine food, yet gulp down their meals. Some choose to lie on the beach their entire lives. Although entitled to choose their path, such people are trapped by the illusion that the body defines the self.

All materialist quagmires can be boiled down to a single mistaken belief, namely, that pain and pleasure are opposites. It's easy to agree that life is meant for pleasure, so conventional wisdom says: "OK, then let us do all we can to avoid pain." However, the absence of pain does not lead directly to pleasure but rather to comfort. All things being equal, comfort may be a desirable commodity, but it is not pleasure. It is merely the absence of pain or effort.

As we have seen, we need to expend effort to obtain pleasure. Anything in life really worthwhile – good relationships, successful careers, the pursuit of meaning and all of life's lasting pleasures – requires a lot of effort to achieve. If we go after comfort, it is true that we will be rid of pain, but we'll also be robbed of almost any type of achievement. Without effort, there is no real pleasure.

HaRav Noah Weinberg z"tzl used a popular example to illustrate how pain and pleasure are related: He often asked people, "What are parents' greatest pleasure?" Most answer, "Their children."

"Where do parents find their greatest pain?" Everyone gives the same answer, "Their children."

It is no accident that our greatest pleasure is also the thing that takes the greatest amount of effort to achieve. That is the nature of pleasure. Every pleasure in life has a price tag attached to it, namely, the effort. The greater the pleasure, the greater the effort needed to acquire it. Superficial pleasures require far less effort to attain. To truly appreciate each level of pleasure, we have to learn to focus on the pleasure and not on the price we are paying to get that pleasure. If we focus on the pleasure, we hardly notice the effort. But if we focus on the effort, we won't notice the pleasure.

Let's return to the example of basketball, from Chapter Four. Take a group of teenagers who love to play ball. On a *bein hazemanim* (summer vacation) afternoon, they can play continuously for two or three hours. What would happen if we asked them to conduct the following experiment?

Play ball as you would normally, but we are going to take away the ball. We want you to run, jump, shoot and defend against each other as you would if you were really playing.

How long could they continue? After five or ten minutes, they would start wondering, *What is the point? Why are we being put through this exercise?* They would say, "We've had enough of this! Please give the ball back." Give them back the ball, and they will play for another two hours.

Not only do we need a challenge – the basketball, a hoop, an opponent – but the amount of pleasure is directly proportional to the amount of challenge. The mental effort of keeping one's eye on the ball – of focusing on the pleasure – is the essence of connoisseurship. In every category of pleasure, we have a choice: either focus on the pleasure or focus on the effort. Focus on the effort, and we do not even want to get out of bed. Focus on the pleasure, and no amount of effort can deter us.

One of my memorable youthful experiences was a seminar on wine tasting. We learned that wine is far more than fermented grape juice. There is a whole range of pleasures available in every glass. Wine has bouquet, color and texture, and gives a different taste to different parts of the mouth. After learning to enjoy wine, we thought that only barbarians could guzzle a glass.

Life offers incredible opportunities for pleasure. A single flower would give us hours of pleasure if we could sensitize ourselves to all of its exquisite details (Chapter Four). But without learning to appreciate such beauty, a flower gives a lift for a few minutes and then leaves us flat. For each type of pleasure, we have to learn *how* to appreciate the pleasure in order to access it. Just as wine is an acquired taste, every type of pleasure needs cultivation.

Yet cultivation is not enough. The soul may want to sip the wine, but the body is always there with its appetite, eager to guzzle. Just as an unbridled horse will roam freely, the body will do anything to get its version of pleasure. It needs to be reined in and trained to go where the soul wants to go. When the soul guides the body properly, the body becomes a vessel for spirituality, and thus the body becomes elevated.

This process of elevation occurs in minute steps, each of

which is a free-will choice to follow the soul's inclination rather than that of the body. Such choices are where all meaningful effort occurs. It is that very effort – which itself is minutely rarefying the body – that contains all of the pleasure.

The key to remember is that the desires of the body are not there to distract us or to be overcome. They are there to give us real, meaningful (and usually difficult) choices, for it is through the choices that we elevate ourselves. As a rule, the body's materialistic pleasures are those experiences that require no mental effort to achieve and are basically physical-emotional experiences alone. This rule applies to every type of pleasure:

- For instance, aesthetic pleasure (A) requires focus and appreciation; otherwise the experience is a form of gluttony.
- Love (L) requires focus on the beloved's goodness. Otherwise the relationship will vacillate according to variable physical and emotional conditions.
- Goodness/ethics (E) requires the effort of admitting mistakes. Otherwise, one will only be good when conditions allow.
- Great creative expression (C) requires focusing on others. Otherwise, one's creative energy will lead to taking as much as giving, and will depend on one's material and emotional state of being.

In all of these examples, the materialistic urge is more than a red herring: it allows the very choice that makes the experience pleasurable. The materialism provides the fuel to energize the transcendental spiritual experience (T).

Take the aesthetic (A) example of food once again. As much as one may become a gourmet, the pleasure of fine food is significantly diminished without an appetite. But with an appetite, one's entire being can resonate with joy at a fine, gourmet meal.

On the next level (L), physicality can actually reach its fullest depth of expression in a caring relationship.

147

When faced with an ethical (E) choice, it is only the impulse to be bad that makes the choice to be good at all meaningful.

Finally, in the area of creativity/altruism (C), the materialistic impulse to control can be the engine to run an enormous outpouring of altruism – as long as one makes the choice to focus on the needs of others rather than one's own.

In all of these areas, it should be apparent that the actual pleasure is directly proportional to both cultivation (becoming a connoisseur) and effort. This level of detail is necessary because pleasure is serious business! If someone goes into a venture capitalist's office and says, "I have a great idea to help you make ten million dollars. Just invest a few hundred thousand dollars with me to get it going," the VC would not say, "Great. Let's go!" (not lately, anyhow). First the VC would investigate whether or not the deal was for real. This rule applies to any pleasure. We have to make sure that we invest our two most precious resources, time and energy, in pursuit of real, not counterfeit, pleasures.

Recall that this section on effort/pain began with the understanding that life is for pleasure, and that there are different types of pleasure to be had. It bears repeating that spiritual pleasure requires an effort on two levels:

1. Pleasure is proportional to cultivation, so become a connoisseur.
2. Learn to spot the materialistic, counterfeit pleasures. They seduce us into not making the effort for true pleasure. They are the body's attempt to be in control and thus they enable us to make real, meaningful choices.

❧ Pleasure versus Happiness

One of the most revered spiritual leaders in the gentile world, the Dalai Lama, is often quoted as saying, "I believe that the very purpose of life is to be happy." Superficially, it sounds as though Judaism and Tibetan Buddhism are saying the same thing. However, there is a distinction between happiness and pleasure. Happiness refers to a particular state of being that one may or may not reach in this lifetime and in this world. Pleasure refers to a process that leads toward happiness.

A simple example is, once again, a basketball game. The winners are typically happy, the losers unhappy. Yet, the pleasure is experienced almost entirely during the playing of the game. Pleasure is a process that does not depend on a specific outcome.

❧ Why Judaism?

What are the advantages of seeking pleasure through Torah or any system? Would it not be even more pleasurable to invent a new system? The answer is that not all spiritual actions are equally transcendental; many are completely illusory.

This point is easiest to grasp on the moral level. There are few in our society who would defend the act of flying an airplane into a building full of innocent people on grounds of moral relativism. Regardless of what the perpetrators believe, we do not believe that this action will produce even a modicum of transcendence. Why not? Why should that action be any different from feeding orphans? It is as if there is a filter that allows some actions to rise through and others not. Such a filter operates on every level:

- Aesthetically, some sensual experiences are simply not conducive to transcendence. An extreme example is eating people. One may be a connoisseur of human flesh, but no amount of berachos with kavana will help us make that meal a transcendent one.
- In the realm of love, most would agree that intimate love with a parent, a sibling or a friend's spouse will not reach the transcendental plane.
- We already mentioned morality, above. Terrorists are an extreme and easy example. It gets more difficult to identify the parameters of the filter when faced with issues such as: *What is stealing?*
- An example of the filter concept in the area of creativity

might be a case where one tries to help someone who does not want to be helped.

We clearly need a system to tell us which actions can make it across the filter to transcendence and which cannot. Filtering is the primary function of the Torah. The Torah is a representation, encoded in story form, of this primordial filter between Infinite Creator and finite you.

All that remains, then, is to learn it.

✒ The Pleasure Virtuoso

Imagine that someone tells you, "We have a little room back here. You can sit down and speak to the Almighty Himself for a whole hour." For many people, would that not be the ultimate? The greatest pleasure, categorically above everything else, is to be one with God; to unite your own infinite spark with the Source of all goodness and pleasure; to have such a keen awareness of Hashem's presence that everything you do is accompanied by a sense of His love and guidance. That is the greatest pleasure.

To get it we have to pay a great price, to make an incredible effort. The price is actually economical, though. It does not require growing your hair long or cutting it short. It does not require quitting your job or changing your lifestyle. The greatest pleasure is spiritual and has a spiritual price: *gratitude*. In order to connect to God with love, one must learn to appreciate all the good that He has done. That means giving up the illusion that we alone are responsible for everything we have achieved and admitting that everything we have is a gift from God.

This is a very difficult awareness to sustain, because a human being's ego always craves recognition and independence; it balks at the concept of indebtedness to a "Higher Power." A person always prefers to believe that he has done everything by himself. If, however, one makes the effort to recognize and appreciate the uncountable wonders that the Infinite Creator has given us, we learn to sense His presence in every aspect of our lives. We should be

overwhelmed by the good that He has bestowed upon us and we
should achieve a transcendence that begets a pleasure far above
any of the four categories below it. The greatest pleasure is the
intensely rewarding experience of closeness to Hashem. This experience is the ultimate goal for which humanity was created.

Focus on what you are living for. Work at it. You are here for
pleasure, but it is good, hard work. It is hard work to be a champion Olympic runner, and even harder work to use all of our tools
to become a champion human being. But that's the only way to
get all the pleasures. You were not born to be comfortable. You
were born to have pleasure – the greatest pleasure. Just as we want
only the best for our children, the Infinite Giver does not intend
anything less for us.

LEVEL	PLEASURE	COUNTERFEIT	EFFORT
1	Transcen-dence	Idolatry (false "gods")	Appreciation (amazement)
2a	Creativity	Power/control	Taking responsibility
2b	Ethics	Looking good/ "success"	Accountability (admit mistakes)
3	Love	Infatuation	Commitment
4	Aesthetics	Gluttony	Self-discipline

This chart shows the hierarchy of pleasures, along with their counterfeit forms and the effort involved in getting the real thing. The
chart contains a serious conceptual flaw, however, for although
infinite pleasure – the pleasure of a relationship with Hashem – is

indeed qualitatively higher than the others since it is infinite, yet despite the hierarchy, it is actually available from any of the other levels.

For instance, in order to enjoy food qua food – to enjoy the aesthetic experience of food – I need to slow down, notice the details and savor. But if, in addition to that sensory enjoyment, I appreciate that this food comes from the Infinite Source and that it is a gift to me, then I can instantly transform the pleasure of eating into infinite pleasure. That appreciation is another word for kavana and is the incredible nature of infinite pleasure – it is readily accessible at all times.

Therefore, to capture this transcendental potential within every category of pleasure in the hierarchy, we have used the "wave" diagram:

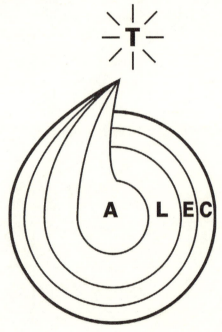

The only problem with the wave is that it implies that any aesthetic, loving, ethical or intellectual pleasure could also become transcendental, with the input of a little appreciation or amazement. Yet we demonstrated above that there exists some kind of filter that allows some actions with kavana to truly transcend while others fail. Therefore, a more representative diagram would show that filter as well as what is on the other side.

Thus, the letter *aleph* can represent this process. The scriptural *aleph* consists of two *yud* letters separated by a *vav*. *Vav* in Hebrew means "and"; it is always a link between two things. In this case, the *vav* represents a filter as well. The *yud* below is pointing upward while the *yud* above points downward, for just as we strive towards transcendence, Hashem seeks a relationship with us, as it were, for that is the purpose of creation.

The three letters that make up the *aleph*, namely two *yuds* and one *vav*, have the gematria (numerical value) of 26, the same as that of the ineffable four-letter name. The *aleph* itself has a gematria of one. This represents the ultimate message of the *Shema*. It also alludes to the true harmony of heaven and earth that humanity alone can create through harmonious thought, speech and action:

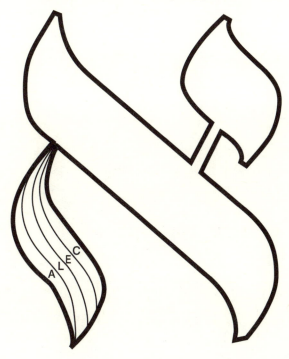

- *Thought* can clarify ideas and seek truth *but* tends to wander and be lazy;
- *speech*, used well, can focus the emotions *but* tends to be used carelessly, adversely affecting the mind;
- *action* can focus and reinforce the thoughts *but* tends to be lazy and disconnected from the mind.

The realm of action will require a subsequent volume to elucidate. May the present volume be a useful step of the grand kavana challenge that readers find before them.

Acknowledgments

To list all the *rebbe'im* who taught me to learn and to love learning would run this book over its page limit. Others who have aided and abetted the process of producing this series of books are too numerous to mention. Thank you for your significant critical feedback and unending encouragement.

Thank you especially to my family. My father, of blessed memory, and my mother taught me from a very young age to cultivate the present moment and to love all kinds of learning. My wife has been my complete partner in this labor of love. And our children will hopefully forgive me yet one more creative pleasure at their expense.

During the creative process, it is natural for the artist to take credit. It takes effort to appreciate where appreciation is due. This attempt to grasp a tiny portion of *Toras Emes* (truthful teachings) has taught me much more than these pages can convey, and I am deeply grateful to HaKadosh Baruch Hu for the inspiration and wherewithal.

About the Author

Alexander Seinfeld received *semicha* from Harav Zalman Nehemia Goldberg, *shlita*, and two degrees from Stanford University.

He founded Jewish Spiritual Literacy, Inc., a non-profit organization dedicated to promoting the ideas in this book.

His audio recordings are available at jsli.org and other sites.

Appendix A

Bibliography

Works cited and further readings

Aaron, Rabbi David. *The Endless Light*. New York: Berkeley Trade Paperbacks, 1998.

Bachya, Rabbeinu (Rabbi Bachya ben Joseph ibn Paqua). *Chovot ha-Levavot./Duties of the Heart*. Trans. from the Arabic into Hebrew by Rabbi Yehuda ibn Tibbon and into English by Moshe Hyamson. New York: Feldheim, 1986 (2 vols).

Birnbaum, Mayer. *Pathway to Prayer*. New York: Feldheim, 1997.

Cardozo, Rabbi Nathan Lopes. *A Critique of Western Civilization* (cassette recording). Jerusalem: Bar-On, 1995.

———. *Tefilla* (cassette recording). Jerusalem: Bar-On, 1997.

Dessler, Rabbi Eliyahu E. *Strive For Truth* (*Michtav MeEliyahu*). Trans. Aryeh Carmell. New York: Feldheim, 1978.

Forst, Rabbi Binyami. *The Laws of B'rachos*. New York: Mesorah, 1990.

Kadish, Seth. *Kavvana: Directing the Heart in Jewish Prayer*. Northvale, NJ: Jason Aronson, 1997.

Kahn, Rabbi Ari D. *Explorations*. Southfield, MI: Targum, 2001.

Kaplan, Rabbi Aryeh. *Jewish Meditation*. New York: Schocken, 1985.

———. *Meditation and the Bible*. York Beach, ME: Samuel Weiser, 1978.

Kelemen, Rabbi Lawrence. *Permission to Believe: Four Rational Approaches to the Torah's Divine Origin*. Southfield, MI: Targum, 1996.

Kirzner, Yitzchok. *The Art of Jewish Prayer*. Northvale, NJ: Aronson, 1991.

Liadi, Rabbi Schneur Zalman. *Likutei Amarim Tanya* (Bilingual Edition). New York: Kehot, 1998.

Lunzano, Rabbi Menachem. *Derech Chayim*. A modern reprint of a section of *Shetei Yados*, 1618.

Luzzatto, Rabbi Moshe Chayim. *Daas Tevunos/The Knowing Heart: The Philosophy of God's Oneness*. Trans. Shraga Silverstein. New York: Feldheim, 1982.

———. *Derech Hashem/The Way of God*. Trans. Aryeh Kaplan. New York: Feldheim, 1977.

———. *Mesillas Yesharim/Path of the Just*. Trans. Shraga Silverstein. New York: Feldheim, 1966.

Mozeson, Isaac E. *The Word: The Dictionary That Reveals the Hebrew Sources of English*. Northvale, NJ: Jason Aronson, 1995.

Munk, Michael L. *The Wisdom in the Hebrew Alphabet: The Sacred Letters as a Guide to Jewish Deed and Thought*. New York: Mesorah, 1993.

Pincus, Rabbi Shimshon David. *Sha'arim BeTefilla: Hera'ot veHasbarim al Asarat Sugei haTefilla HaMuzkarim beChazal*. Ofakim, Israel: Pinchus Family, 5761/2000–2001.

Pliskin, Rabbi Zelig. *Consulting the Wise: Simulated Interviews With Great Torah Scholars of Previous Generations*. New York: Bnei Yakov, 1991.

Seinfeld, Alexander. *The Art of Amazement*. New York: Penguin, 2005.

Soloveitchik, Rabbi Joseph B. *Halachic Man*. Trans. Lawrence Kaplan. Philadelphia: Jewish Publication Society, 1991.

Tatz, Rabbi Dr. Akiva. *World Mask*. Southfield, MI: Targum Press, 1995.

Verman, Mark, *The Histories and Varieties of Jewish Meditation*. Northvale, NJ: Jason Aronson, 1996.

Appendix B

The Exchange

A few days before Rosh Hashana 5768, I received an email from a stranger. He was the director of Jewish studies at a certain Orthodox Jewish day school in a major metropolitan area in the United States. Here is his message verbatim:

> *Rabbi, I have had your book – Art of Amazement – since it was published with the blue cover in 2002.*
>
> *To be frank (as we approach the Yamim Noraim) I have never been able to use it because I felt very strongly that it was, partially, lifted from Tich Nhat Hanh's – Peace is Every Step.'*
>
> *Can you explain the relationship – for example – of the 7-minute orange and his teaching children to eat a tangerine. Is there some Buddhist text that you are both drawing on or are you culling from his book?*
>
> *If it is the latter I think it is a real shame that you aren't mentioning him. I also think there is an implicit halakhic problem... You can be your own judge.*
>
> *Your thoughts are welcome,*
> *Rabbi _____*

This is a serious accusation. Plagiarism is the worst crime a writer can commit. But he accused me of worse than plagiarism – he accused me of teaching something non-Jewish in my book!
Here is how I responded:

Dear Rabbi_____,

Thank you so much for your message. The fact that it took you so long to write and the content of your message suggests that it was not easy for you to broach this subject and I appreciate it and salute you for it.

I will tell you the truth: I have never read Hanh's book, nor have I to my recollection ever held one of his books in my hands, nor could I even name one of his books if you'd asked me. I see that his book was first published in 1992; the last time I opened a Buddhist text was circa 1988 (with the exception of fact-checking for my footnotes when writing this book). So I cannot explain the similarities that you mention.

I rue my own ignorance, because referencing him in Chapter Four or Five or the appendix may have made the book stronger and more credible to one or two Bu-Jews out there.

Every teaching in the book (and in the related classes that I give around the country), to the best of my knowledge, is 100 percent Jewish from universally recognized Jewish sources. There is absolutely no ideological influence of Buddhism or any other "ism" in the book; however, the language is often borrowed from them. The book has unpublished haskamos of Rabbi _____ and Rabbi _____ (who read it quite closely) among others. Judaica Press, which has the strictest standards of "kashrus", offered to distribute the original self-published edition and pulled out when their posek saw the reference in the Introduction to my own personal experience with Buddhism and felt that some young impressionable Jew may read that as a legitimization of such a journey – but they loved the content.

It is interesting that your radar picked up the 7-Minute Orange in particular, because since writing the book I have learned from firsthand witnesses that both HaRav Shach and HaRav Yaakov Weinberg, zichronam leveracha, used a nearly identical technique to teach basic mindful appreciation to young people.

No, this book is Judaism through and through, and if Mr. Hanh or anyone else discovered the same wisdom, well "Baruch shenasan michachmaso lebasar vedam."

Here is a recent comment from a self-described Bu-Jew:

"I have had your book for a while and re-discovered it again this week – on a totally different level:) Shared it with a Bu-Jew (more like Yogi-Jew) friend at work – he is reading it and likes it so much that I ordered another copy for myself)."

And here is a recent comment from a self-described Orthodox Jew:

"My wife and I really enjoyed your inspirational book – we are now on our second reading and find it deepens our everyday life experience – as well as our shul experience during prayers."

Here is an email I received about five minutes ago:

"Hello. I bought your book, 'The Art of Amazement' at the past AJOP convention and want to give it to a friend /talmida who is off to Bhutan (!) now that borders are open. I contacted a book store who told me it is no longer available. How can I get it and how much will it cost? I could give her my copy but…it no longer looks new and I would like[to keep] it. She is well grounded yet a highly sensitive spiritually…she is an [sic] very accomplished person with unique sensitivities to people and the world, and is beginning to drift towards other forms of spirituality. I care about her! Your book, I feel would speak to her."

As you may know, there is a more recent edition published by Penguin which has been considerably improved (including one or two changes in language at Rabbi _____'s request).

Thank you again for breaking the ice. I hope we can meet sometime, here, there, or better in Yerushalyim habenuya.

Ketiva vechatima tova,
Alexander Seinfeld

I have reproduced this email exchange for the reader to consider the state of Jewish education today. That a director of Judaics at an Orthodox Jewish day school could write such a letter, that he could for five years refuse to use the Art of Kavana approach to Judaism because he thought it plagiarized a Vietnamese Buddhist monk, is deeply troubling.

No less disturbing, a veteran fourth-grade teacher at a To-rah U'Mesorah *cheder* told me that he is not inspired to teach the boys any kavanos in the first beracha of the Amida (Avos) because "well, it's a little dry." Yet he wonders why many of the boys seem distracted, looking around the room, during tefilla.

How do we fix this problem?

Major Types of Jewish "Meditation"*

NAME	MEANING	GOAL	METHOD
higayon/ hagig/ hagus/ haga	"Mantra:"	"State of pure existence": nullification of the ego	Vocal repetition of sounds, words, phrases, melodies. Often stage between levels of *rina*
hisbodedut	Isolation w. analytical introspection	Self-awareness	In daily isolation, ask oneself a set of penetrating questions
hisbonenus	Contem-plation	Appreciation of relationship to Hashem	Let the object guide the mind

hispalel/ amida	Self-examining/ "standing" meditation	Re-align one's will to the Infinite will	Daily repetition of a long "mantra" in deep concentration
*ranan/ rina***	Explosive emotions that result in song	Bind to Hashem with all emotions	Often used to prepare for *haga*, then return to *rina* at a higher level
shasha	Enraptured attention	Tranquility	Contemplating Torah, w. oscillating concentration
Shema	*No translation*	Internalize Infinite unity	Said morning and eve, to frame the day
siach	One-pointed introspection	Spiritual growth	Exploration of spiritual worlds
suach	One-pointed introspection	Full spiritual maturity	An ultimate consciousness via *siach*

* Based on Rabbi Aryeh Kaplan, *Meditation and the Bible*.

Appendix D

Prophecy

PREREQUISITES:

Prophecy only occurs to a sage who is great in wisdom, mighty in deeds and whom the material inclination does not control in any material thing; rather he continually fortifies his mind against his inclination and he is an exceedingly masterful intellect.

– Rambam, *Yesodei HaTorah* 7:1

DESCRIPTION OF THE EXPERIENCE:

There are many levels of prophecy. Just as one person may have greater intelligence than another, so one prophet can be greater in prophecy than another.

Yet all of them, rather than seeing a vision, they see their prophecy only in a dream or vision at night, or else during the day, while in a trance....

All of them, while experiencing prophecy, the limbs tremble, the body becomes weak, and they lose control of their stream of consciousness. All that remains in their conscious mind is a clear understanding of what they are experiencing at the time....

The information transmitted to a prophet in a prophetic vision is transmitted to him via allegory. The interpretation of the allegory, however, is immediately implanted in the prophet's mind, and he is aware of its meaning. Like the ladder that Yaakov Avinu saw and the angels ascending and descending on it.

– ibid. 7:2–3

HOW TO ACHIEVE PROPHECY:

The first step in prophecy is a strong desire. This is followed by meditation, which is its means. The goal is then the influx that comes to him.

– Rabbi Yitzchak Abarbanel, *Shmuel I*, 10:5

The prophets would meditate on the highest mysteries.... They would depict these things in their mind with their imaginative faculty, visualizing them as if they were actually in front of them.

When their souls became attached to the Supernal Soul, this vision would be increased and intensified. It would then be revealed automatically through a state where thought is utterly absent.

– Rabbi Menachem Recanti *Peirush* on *VaYechi*, 37d

THERE WERE VARIOUS METHODS:

One must learn these methods from a master.... They would... have to put themselves in a joyous mood.... They would then meditate according to their knowledge of the meditative methods. Through this, they would attain wondrous levels, divesting themselves of the physical, and making the mind overcome the body completely. The mind becomes so overpowering that the physical senses are abandoned and the prophet does not sense anything with them at all.

– Rabbi Moshe Cordevero, *Shiur Komah* 16

Appendix E

The Seven-Minute Orange

This seven-minute version of Chapter Five may be given to anyone – children or adults – who would enjoy improving their sense of amazement and their kavana. Try it with any sweet fruit in season.

Introduction

One of the main reasons that Jewish people do not get more into learning Torah is that it seems inherently impractical. The Torah is full of interesting stories, but "it's not going to help me be successful at work or in my relationships, right?"

The Exercise

To illustrate just how practical the Torah can be, today I'm going to show you what it says about how to eat an orange:

Give each person a whole mandarin orange, one segment of a navel orange, a knife, a plate, a napkin.

Now, each person should have a whole orange and a single segment. To begin, please enjoy the single segment, right now, but do not eat the whole orange!

Make sure every person is eating his segment.

Now, the art of eating an orange, according to Judaism, is really the art of orange appreciation. Please hold up the whole orange and examine it. Notice its **texture**, how it looks and feels. Is it heavy or light?

Pause.

Smell it.

Pause.

How does it smell?

Have you ever noticed on an orange tree how these delightful globules stand out in contrast to the green leaves, just begging to be picked?

Please take your knife and cut the orange into quarters. Does the **smell** change?

Hold up one quarter. Imagine you are an alien from outer space and landed here on earth on a really hot day and you are quite thirsty, and someone said, "Have one of these."

Hold it up as if offering it to someone.

Would you know which part to bite into?

Usually they say no, in which case you continue.

Isn't the inside so much more juicy and inviting than the rind?

Pause for effect.

Smell it again

Pause.

Now I have another question. What's this orange mostly made of?

> *Pause.*

Obviously, it's water. Probably at least 90 percent water. But go like this...

> *You flip your piece over so that the flesh is facing down and the rind is on top – wait for them all to copy you.*

Why doesn't all the liquid fall out? After all, we've cut it open!

> *Pause for effect. Inspect the orange closely and say:*

If you **examine** it closely, you'll notice that it is actually made of tiny little sacs that hold the juice. It's amazing!

Now, I'm going to ask a really practical, straightforward question. I'm looking for a practical, straightforward answer; don't get weird on me, OK? How did so much water get into this form? In other words, if I were to give you a bucket of water, how could you transform it into some of these?

> *Hopefully, someone will figure out that you need to plant a seed and water it; if not, just remind them that this is how we make oranges.*

But we don't generally water orange groves from buckets, do we? Even if we do, where does that water come from? Answer: the rain.

Where does the rain come from? Answer: evaporation.

What causes evaporation? Answer: the sun.

Where does the sun get its energy? Answer: left over from the big bang.

Now, when it comes to the big bang, science has to stop, because anything before that is unobservable and immeasurable. But according to Judaism, before the big bang, there was an Infinite God who created from nothing. What you have, therefore, is a direct chain of cause and effect from God to this orange in your hand! Are you starting to appreciate what an amazing gift this is? It's literally a gift!

One last question: We're all on a board together. Imagine that this were the Ford Foundation, and I walked in here today, held up one of these oranges slices and said, "Ladies and gentlemen, I know what I want to fund next year. I want to fund the research to produce these things from scratch in the laboratory." How much are we going to have to invest to make it happen? Answer: billions…or impossible!

Yet, you can buy them literally for pennies! And today you're eating it for free! What did you do to deserve such a wonderful gift? Were you extra nice to someone today?

Now, to eat your second piece of orange, please close your eyes, think about all the wonderful qualities of this orange, where it ultimately comes from, how it is literally and figuratively a gift (and how you don't even deserve to be eating it, so to speak), and now bite into the orange, keep your eyes closed, and let it roll over your tongue, really taste it and take your time before you swallow.

> *Give them a long time – if you want, while they're eating, you can tell them a piece of orange trivia – in Florida, most of the oranges are grown for juicing and in California, for eating, and they make jokes about each other's oranges. In Florida, they say that you could run over a California orange with a steamroller and not even get the pavement wet. In California, they say that if you want to eat a Florida orange you have to sit in the bathtub.*

How did the second bite compare?

> *You can ask for a show of hands for who enjoyed the second eating more than the first.*

Judaism teaches that – yes, your mother was right, slow down and chew your food – that every bite of food we eat every day, and everything else in this world, we should experience with that kind of intense focus and appreciation.

What about when we have difficulties in life, trials and tribulations? Any thoughts?

> *Chances are, no one will get it, but someone may.*
> *pause*

Who would Michael Jordan rather play one-on-one – Magic Johnson or…*dramatic pause with a mock-pride smile – say your name and point to yourself with mock smugness*?

Why would he obviously want to play Magic? Wouldn't he beat me so much more easily?

It's obvious, isn't it? Pleasure in life is not the absence of pain! We find pleasure only through challenges, or "pain" as it were. No pain, no gain.

CONCLUSION

There is a lot more to say on this subject, but we're overtime. If you would like to go into this topic in depth, please ask me later and I'll refer you to my rabbi.

But to conclude, does anyone know what the word "Torah" means? Hint: It doesn't mean "Bible"! Answer: It means "instructions." In modern Hebrew, for instance, *torat nehiga* means "driving instructions"; *torat bayit* means "home economics" – what kind of instructions is *the Torah*?

[Someone will guess – "For life?"]

That's right – Torat/Toras Chaim, instructions for living. Our challenge as Jews is to maintain the life in our Torah as much as it is to maintain the Torah in our life, for we are the p‿ople who have kept the Torah alive for millennia, and the Torah is arguably what has defined us a people for so long.

Note to teacher: Depending on your audience, it is wonderful but not always necessary to quote directly from the Torah. Nevertheless, appreciating life in spite of the challenges is a major theme of many chapters in the Torah. Therefore, one may wish to use this class as a D'var Torah on the weekly portion.

Appendix F

More Berachos

The following list of berachos is part of the traditional morning warm-up. They are listed here according to the customary order. Each beracha begins:

"BORUCH ATOH (BARUCH ATA) ADONOI ELOHEINU MELECH HO-OLOM (HA-OLAM…"

> *You are the Source – the Infinite (beyond all space and time) – our power, the director of the concealment…*

KAVANA	BERACHA
That I can hold it in and let it out!	…*asher yotzar es ho-odom bechochmoh, uvoro vo nekovim nekovim, chaluleem chaluleem. Golui veyodua lifnei kisei kevodechoh she'im yifosei'ach echod meihem oh yisoseim echod meihem, ee-efshar lehiska-yeim vela'a-mohd lifone-choh afilu sho-oh echos. Boruch atoh Adonoi, rofei chol bo-sor umaflee la'asos.* (…Who made the human being wisely and created within

176

	him/her many holes and cavities. It is revealed and known in the highest realms that if just one were opened or just one were stopped up it would be impossible to continue and to stand for before You for even one hour. You, the Infinite, are the Source, healing all flesh and doing amazing things.)
That I am consciousness!	…asher nosan lesech-vee vee-noh, lehav-cheen bein yom u-vein loi-loh. (…giving understanding to the rooster to distinguish between day and night.)
That I have eyes to see!	…po-kei-ach ivreem. (…giving sight to the blind.)
That I have clothes!	…malbeesh arumeem (clothes the naked).
That I can move freely!	…mateer asureem (releases the bound).
That I can stand upright!	…zokeif kefu-feem (straightens the bent).
That I have firm ground on which to walk!	…roka ho-oretz al ha-moi-im (spreads the land over the water).
That I have shoes!	…sheh-osoh lee kol tzor-chee (Who took care of all my needs).
That I can walk!	…asher-heicheen mitzadei go-ver (strengthens a person's footsteps).
That I'm a Yisrael with inner dignity!	…o-zeir Yisro-eil bigevuroh (empowers a Yisrael).
That I am aware of the Almighty!	…oteir Yisroel beseef-oroh (crowns Yisrael with splendor).
That I am able to be active today!	…ha-nosein la-yo-ayf koach. (Who gives strength to the weary).

Index

A

Adam
    as first prophet, 62
    as model for male-female re-
        lationship, 79, 125, 128
    and power of berachos, 86–87
Amida (see Kavana, Amida)
appreciation, 35
    as a result of contempla-
        tion, 47, 57, 172, 174
    as a measure of tran-
        scendence, 58
    constant, 58-60, 68, 140
    for others, 75
    as the source of love, 89
    for one's own goodness, 103, 115
    required for aesthetic
        pleasure, 147
    as key to kavana, 151–152
art of kavana
    ancient schools (see proph-
        ecy, training schools)
    as a constant practice, 13,
        40, 48-50, 66, 140
    benefits of, 88 (see
        also deveikus)
    benefits of even mini-
        mal practice, 50
    introduced, 2–5
    effort required, 56
    need for a guide, 13
    need for balanced practice, 61
Arizal, 26, 121
atomic theory, 17
Avraham
    historic figure, 7, 18, 28, 100
    as liturgical symbol, 124,
        125, 129–131
    and Sarah, 7, 28, 125, 129, 130

B

Ba'al Shem Tov, 107, 133
berachos, 12, 63–69, 86, 116–117,
    122-125, 140, 149, 177, 179

C

contemplation
    as a meditation (see medi-
        tation, hisbonenus)
    and appreciating pain, 59
    and Shabbos, 95

D

Dalai Lama, 148
Dessler, Rabbi Eliyahu,
　　　viii, 24, 25, 159
deveikus, xvii, 3, 13, 28, 40,
　　　50–51, 53-55, 59-64
　　defined, 38, 50, 53, 121, 144
　　and Hebrew, 62-63
　　and Berachos, 64, 116
　　and the Sh'ma, 82, 86, 88
　　and goodness, 101, 111
　　and the Amida, 120, 133

E

eating (see kavana in eating)
Einstein, Albert, 16–17

F

Feinstein, Rabbi. Moshe, 67, 104
First Temple, 5, 6, 11, 42, 116

G

gematria
　　and love, 79, 123
　　and the Amida, 116
　　and aleph, 152–153
gilgul (reincarnation), 121, 144
goodness
　　and human purpose, 27, 33
　　as Divine essence, 26, 150
　　as pleasure, 99
　　as root of love, 75, 147
　　cultivating, 102-106
　　defined, 101
　　verses greatness, 107-109
　　God, (see Infinite)
Greenland, 10

H

Hawking, Stephen, 17, 22, 67
happiness, 8, 27–28, 108

　　see also: pleasure v. happiness
Hebrew
　　as ultimate deveikus lan-
　　　guage, 62-63
　　decline of knowledge of, 62-65
hisbodedus (see meditation,
　　hisbodedus)
hisbonenus (see medita-
　　tion, hisbonenus)
how to eat a piece of fruit, 56
Hubble, Edwin, 16–17

I

Infinite (God)
　　and berachos, 64–66, 69–70, 87
　　as Creator, 18, 26, 31, 113, 173
　　as unknowable, 54
　　definition of, 17–18,
　　　22–23, 26, 31, 54
　　and definition of Yisrael, 31
　　and deveikus, 40, 50, 51, 53, 85
　　distinction between Infi-
　　　nite and infinity, 23
　　and giving, 115
　　and goodness,
　　light analogy for, 45
　　mitzvah of loving, 43
　　and prayer, 119–122, 124,
　　　127, 131-134, 139,
　　and prophesy (see prophesy)
　　and purpose, 27, 86
　　relationship to fi-
　　　nite, 24–27, 54, 95
　　and the Sh'ma, 89
　　and the soul, 35, 37, 86, 144, 150
　　as source, 56, 58, 64
　　as ultimate pleasure, 152
　　understanding, 19–22

J

Judaism, 149–150
　　purpose of, 28–29

K

Kabbala, 3, 26, 27, 81, 110
  defined, 12,
Kaplan, Rabbi Aryeh, 6, 81,
      107, 108, 160, 168
karma, 57, 80, 85, 87, 101,
      113, 121, 122, 132
  defined, 121
kavana
  definition of, xvi
  as meditation, 9–11
  as solution to body-soul
      problem, 34–39, 105
  exercises for develop-
      ing, 49–51, 69, 91, 103, 137
  feedback loop of, 90
  in Baruch Sheim Kavod, 84–88
  in brachos, 63–68
  in eating, 56–59
  in ethics, 103
  in relationships, 80
  in the Shema, 80–95
  in Tefilla (Amida), 119–132
    alone versus with
        group, 139–141
    first beracha of, 124–132
    goal of, 124
    as agent of change, 133
    as meditation on his-
        tory, 138–139
    location and time, 134–135
    position, 134
    technique, 133–134
    voice, 136
    warm-up and warm-
        down, 135–136
  preparation for (see
      washing hands)
  and prophecy, 6, 40–42
  transcendental, 60
Ketura, 7

Knesses HaGedola
    (Sanhedrin), 63–65, 68, 116

L

Lapland, 10
Leah. 120–131
love
  defined, 73–75
  and intimacy, 95–96

M

Maimonides, see Rambam
marriage, 3, 76
  ideal, 79, 95, 125–126
meditation
  chart, 167–168
  community, 94–95
  defined, 9–12
  practices (see kavana)
    hisbodedus (intro-
        spection), 108
    hisbonenus (contem-
        plation), 46–48
    Life (see Kavana in Tefilla)
    Shema (see Kavana
        in the Shema)
meditatzia, 9
Midrash, 6, 7, 28, 87
Milky Way, 19
minyan (see Kavana: in Tefilla:
    (alone versus with group)
morality, Ch. 7
  how to cultivate, improve,
      fix mistakes, 104–106
  how to go from "good" to
      "great", 108–110
  "I'm wrong" and "I'm
      sorry", 105–106
  objective standards, 109-110
  standards depend on in-
      dividual, 104
  transcendental, 110–111

mussar, (see morality)
music, 5, 8, 9, 39, 47, 48, 59,
      65, 93, 94, 114, 135

N

nevi'im, (see prophets)

P

patience, 103, 133
pleasure
    chart (wave), 39, 152
    table, 151
    versus happiness, 148–149
    versus pain, 50-60, 143-148
    virtuoso, 150-135
prayer, 8
    Amida as, 119-122
    defined, 80
    how to get answered, 122
    verses mantra, 81
    within the Amida, 133
prophecy, 41 (see also ka-
    vana, and prophecy)
    description and tech-
    niques, 169–170
    training schools, 42
prophets, number of, 42
purpose of life, 27–28

R

Rachel, 129–131
Rambam, 12, 15, 40, 43, 57, 61, 91, 169
Ramban, 7, 50, 64
religions of the East, 3, 7, 94, 119, 125
reincarnation, (see gilgul)
ritual, 44–46
Rivka, 129–130

S

Sanhedrin, (see Knesses HaGedola)
Sarah, (see Avraham and Sarah)

as complement to Avra-
    ham, 130
as great teacher, 7
as greater prophet than
    Avraham, 125, 141
Schroeder, Dr. Gerald, 30
Shabbos (Shabbat), 93–95
    defined, 95
Sheim (school of), 6–7
Shema (see Kavana in the Shema)
    contrasted with Amida, 117
Shlomo Hamelech, 134
snow, words for, 10–12
speech, power of, 62
spiritual (spirituality)
    attraction, 77
    awareness, 62
    benefits of, 24, 45,
    81, 90 (ff), 114
    decline, 11, 63-64
    defined, 8-9, 34-35,
    119, 139-140
    example of, 104, 130-131, 148
    error, 85, 149
    and gender, 125-131
    journey, 2-5, 30, 40, 44,
    49, 61, 85, 102-103, 141
    mature v. immature, 103
    potential, 108, 128-129, 146
    pleasures, 28-30,
    35-40, 148-153
    rest, 95
    speech, 80
    verses material, 34
success, 106, 151

T

Tanya (Sefer), 26, 71, 82
tefilla, (see Kavana, tefilla)
terrorism, 98-100
Torah (Toras Chayim)
    definition of, 109, 175

first mitzva in, 29
shebe'al peh (Oral Torah), 110
spiritual path of, 55
transcendence, 50–51, 58, 84, 96, 116,
        123, 134, 138, 139, 149–152
    as goal of tefila, 124, 129
    as invention of Avraham, 131
    as mida of Yitzchak, 129
tzaddik (tzedeikis), 5, 121
tzimtzum, 26

U

universe, size of, 19–20

V

voice, using, 62, 64, 84, 136

W

washing hands, 43–46

Y

Yaakov
    historic figure, 6–7, 31, 82
    as liturgical symbol, 129, 131
Yitzchak
    historic figure, 6
    as liturgical symbol, 129–131
yin-yang, 113, 125–129, 141
wave chart, (see pleasure chart)

Z

Zohar, 5, 6, 26, 27